LEAVING CERT **BUSINESS**

THE HIGHER OPTION

By Philip Curry

First published in 2020
by Philip Curry

ISBN 978-1-8381744-0-8

Book design and layout by
SiobhanFoody.com

CONTENTS

EXAM **PLAN**

Time	Exam Plan
9:30	**Read The Paper And Do All SAQs**
10:00	**ABQ**
10:40	**First Long Question**
11:05	**Second Long Question**
11:30	**Third Long Question**
11:55	**Fourth Long Question**
12:20	**Final Sweep Of Paper**

Short Answer Questions (SAQs)

20% of the Higher Level Paper

Advice:

✔ 'Over answer' the definitions questions
✔ Always label diagrams
✔ Write true or false in FULL
✔ Use examples when required
✔ Answer all 10 questions

USEFUL
ACRONYMS

AGM:	Annual General Meeting
APR:	Annual Percentage Rate
AOB:	Any Other Business
ATM:	Automated Teller Machine
BEP:	Break Even Point
BIK:	Benefit In Kind
CAP:	Common Agricultural Policy
CCPC:	Competition and Consumer Protection Commission
CEO:	Chief Executive Officer
CFF:	Cash Flow Forecast
CFP:	Common Fisheries Policy
CGT:	Capital Gains Tax
CPI:	Consumer Price Index
CRO:	Companies Registration Office
DAC:	Designated Activity Company
DIRT:	Deposit Interest Retention Tax
ECJ:	European Court of Justice
ERDF:	European Regional Development Fund
EDI:	Electronic Data Interchange
EGM:	Extraordinary General Meeting
EPOS:	Electronic Point Of Sale
EMU:	Economic and Monetary Union
ESF:	European Social Fund
FDI:	Foreign Direct Investment
GDPR:	General Data Protection Regulation
HRM:	Human Resource Management
IBEC:	Irish Business and Employers Confederation
ICT:	Information Communications Technology
ICTU:	Irish Congress of Trade Unions
IDA:	Industrial Development Authority
IFA:	Irish Farmers Association
ISME:	Irish Small and Medium Sized Enterprise
ISO:	International Standards Organisation
JIT:	Just-in-time
LEO:	Local Enterprise Office
MBO:	Management Buy Out
MNC:	Multinational Company
PAYE:	Pay As You Earn
PLC:	Public Limited Company
PPSN:	Personal Public Service Number
PR:	Public Relations
PRO:	Public Relations Officer
PRSI:	Pay Related Social Insurance
R&D:	Research and Development
ROCE:	Return On Capital Employed
ROI:	Return On Investment
SEM:	Single European Market
SWOT:	Strengths, Weaknesses, Opportunities, Threats
TNC:	Transnational Company
TQM:	Total Quality Management
USC:	Universal Social Charge
VAT:	Value Added Tax
WCM:	World Class Manufacturing
WRC:	Workplace Relations Commission
WTO:	World Trade Organisation

THE **A–Z** OF BUSINESS DEFINITIONS

→ The following is a very useful list of core definitions as per the Business syllabus
→ The **bolded** words are keywords to the definition
→ The advice in the margins is also very important

Term	Meaning	Unit
Acid test ratio	Used to measure cash flow in a business. Its formula is: Current Assets – Closing Stock ————————————————— Current Liabilities Ideally the answer should be 1:1, which means that for every euro that **falls due in the short-term**, there is one euro to meet it.	Unit 4
Acquisition	The overall term for procuring another business. It is the purchase of one company by another. E.g. The purchase of Jurys Inn by Lone Star Funds for €911m.	Unit 5
Advertising	The communication of information about a product or service to the general public in the hope of selling the good or service. It can inform, persuade or remind.	Unit 5
Agenda	A list of items to be dealt with at a meeting – the agenda should be relevant to those at the meeting.	Unit 3
Agreement	The first element of contract law. One party makes a proposal to give or do something – which is called an offer – and the other party replies with a positive, unqualified assent to all terms of the offer. This is called acceptance.	Unit 1
Arbitration	A method of solving conflict between parties. An independent party acts like a referee and listens to both sides of the argument before the arbitrator (referee) finds an independent solution to the dispute. E.g. An arbitrator's solution was rejected by the Association of Secondary Teachers of Ireland, as it offered less than the original pay claim.	Unit 1
Articles of association	The internal rules and regulations of a company. Contains details of the following: • Share capital breakdown • Voting rights attached to each share • Procedure for calling a meeting	Unit 6
Batch production	The making of a limited group of identical goods. The goods are in various sizes. Production is interrupted and goods are kept in stock. E.g. tins of beans.	Unit 5

Branding	The use of a legally registered name as a trademark, which gives exclusive rights to the owner. A brand creates a myth of superiority in the consumers' mind, which means that the consumer is willing to pay more for the good or service.	Unit 5
Break-even	A production position where the firm makes neither a profit nor a loss i.e. total cost = total revenue It is part of product pricing.	Unit 5
Business plan	A document which maps out a business future under a series of headings. It guides the firm towards its targets. It is used to attract investors.	Unit 5
Capacity to contract	This contract element is the power of a natural person to enter into a contract. It means being legally able to enter a contract. Persons under 18 do not have this power, or people who are not of sound mind, or those under the influence of alcohol or illegal drugs.	Unit 1
Cash flow forecasts	Cash flows show the difference between money flowing in and money flowing out of a business or household. A forecast shows a firm's cash position in the future.	Unit 5
Categories of industry	Refer to the industrial divisions in an economy i.e. **primary, secondary and tertiary**. In Ireland, the tertiary sector is the most important.	Unit 6
Channel of distribution	Is the means of getting the goods from the producer to the consumer e.g. Manufacturer → Consumer (this is normally used for expensive specialist products e.g. fitted kitchens. This channel is also called direct selling.)	Unit 5
Community enterprise	Refers to the promotion of a proactive and entrepreneurial mentality in the local economy. It reduces the dependence on multinational investment. It uses a bottom-up approach, self-help policy and a social and economic perspective.	Unit 6
Conciliation	This method of conflict resolution is used to solve conflicts in the workplace. An independent third party, usually an Industrial Relations Officer provided by the Workplace Relations Commission, works **with** both parties to facilitate the search for a mutually acceptable solution to end the conflict.	Unit 1
Consideration	This contract element is whatever **benefit** passes between the parties to a contract e.g. consumer receives the goods and the retailer receives the monetary reward. It must be real, transferable, but need not be adequate.	Unit 1
Consumer	A person who uses goods for private purposes to gain personal satisfaction and does not purchase goods for the purpose of re-sale. A consumer aims to satisfy needs and wants within a financial constraint called a budget.	Unit 1

Controlling · **Stock** · **Credit** · **Quality**	The comparison of the results with the original plans, and measuring performance. The firm must take corrective action to deal with deviations, which are affecting objectives. *The firm must:* • Set standards • Compare actual results with plans • Correct deviations • Learn from mistakes	Unit 3
Co-operative relationship **Win-win situation**	This exists where joint action or effort is required to enable people to work and operate together so that there will be mutual benefit e.g. if the entrepreneur has a well-researched idea backed up by a business plan and the investor is impressed and supplies finance for the project then the relationship is co-operative.	Unit 1
Co-operatives **7 members minimum**	Unique, democratic ownership options. Members are workers, suppliers, and customers. There is usually a common interest. They were introduced to Ireland for farm produce.	Unit 6
Co-ordination	The linking together of all the various departments of the organisation to achieve a shared objective. It avoids duplication and prevents conflict in the organisation. It is part of the leadership process.	Unit 3
Council of Ministers	The **main decision-making body** of the EU. It consists of one government minister from each country. Each council represents a different topic, e.g. Council of Agricultural Ministers.	Unit 7
Credit control	Ensures that the firm deals with the right **debtors** (they owe us) and minimises bad debts. It sets levels of credit, e.g. €1,000. It sets time limits, e.g. 60 days. Effective credit control improves cash flow.	Unit 3
Desk research **(Secondary)**	A type of market research whereby the information is already gathered and available, and this makes it a low-cost method. There are both internal and external sources.	Unit 5
Electronic Data Interchange (EDI)	The use of structured documents sent from one computer to another via the telephone system. Businesses need to have compatible systems and it may prove to be expensive for small businesses. It has revolutionised stock control and improved speed and efficiency, and has reduced the paper chain. It reduces the costs of unnecessary overstocking. It is used to transmit money electronically	Unit 3
Empowerment	This is the transfer of real responsibility by the manager of the firm. It places decision-making, control and responsibility in the hands of employees in the organisation. It is an advanced form of delegation.	Unit 4

Enterprise	One of the four factors of production and it involves taking the human initiative and using a moderate degree of risk to combine the factors of production into a business unit. The entrepreneur spots a gap in the market and this is called a niche market.	Unit 2
Equity	The owner's stake in a firm. It consists of **ordinary shares and reserves.**	Unit 5
Ethical business practice	Refers to a set of moral principles that cause a person or firm to act in a certain way. An ethic involves a valued judgement on what is right and what is wrong.	Unit 6
EU directive	Part of the decision-making process of the European Union. It suggests that a law should be changed but leaves it to the member state to implement it, e.g. the Irish government introduced the plastic bag tax in response to an EU directive on waste reduction.	Unit 7
EU policy	An agreed means of achieving agreed objectives, e.g. the Social policy improves the lives of individuals.	Unit 7
European Commission	Made up of 28 commissioners, one from each member state. It initiates legislation for the EU. It also ensures that legislation is applied by all member states.	Unit 7
European Parliament	An elected body of 751 members. It has the power to amend certain laws. It supervises EU community activities and sets up committees to investigate problems in the EU.	Unit 7
European Union	A group of 28 member states with close economic and political ties. It is a trading bloc and has common policies to achieve members' aims.	Unit 7
Exchange rate	The price of one currency in terms of another, e.g. the April 2020 exchange rate is €1 = 88p sterling	Unit 6
Exporting	The process of sending goods and services abroad. The Irish economy is so small that Irish firms must seek markets overseas.	Unit 5
Feasibility study	Allows the firm to look at the impact of the product on the areas of costs, revenues and profits. The demand for sales is forecast, and contribution and breakeven point are established. It also looks at the environmental effects. **It is an investigative report into viability.**	Unit 5

Global marketing ***Know standardised and adapted***	Refers to all the activities in identifying and anticipating the needs and wants of consumers in a single world-wide marketplace. It includes global product, global price, global promotion and global place, e.g. Coca-Cola.	Unit 7
Goals	An entrepreneur's objectives, i.e. what the firm sets out to do. In most cases the entrepreneur wishes to maximise profits.	Unit 2
Grants and subsidies	A grant is a non-repayable source of finance usually given by the government to encourage enterprise and initiative, e.g. feasibility studies and employment grants. A subsidy is a **payment to the producer** to reduce the cost of production, which boosts employment and exports.	Unit 6
Gross margin	This is gross profit measured as a percentage of sales. The formula is: $\dfrac{\text{Gross Profit} \times 100}{\text{Sales}}$ It measures the profit from buying and selling. It varies from industry to industry.	Unit 4
Gross pay	This is an employee's pay before statutory deductions, e.g. PAYE and PRSI, and voluntary deductions, e.g. VHI and Christmas club.	Unit 4
Gross profit	This is a firm's profit made from buying and selling without taking expenses into account. It is calculated by using the following formula: **Sales – Cost of Sales**	Unit 4
Human relations	This involves being good with people, understanding their needs and behaviours, and being able to relate to the people in and around the business. People can do courses in communications and psychology to improve this area.	Unit 2
Imports ***Know both visible and invisible***	Goods and services that are produced in foreign countries but are brought into Ireland to cater for the needs and wants of Irish consumers in the domestic economy, e.g. French wine.	Unit 7
Indemnity	This principle states that there will be no profit from insurance. The insurer attempts to put the insured back in the same position as they were before the accident occurred. E.g. If a secondhand car is stolen and destroyed, the owner does not get a brand new one.	Unit 4
Indigenous firms ***Native firms***	Set up in Ireland by Irish people. Enterprise Ireland is the State sponsored body responsible for these firms. Employment grants are made available to promote the spirit of enterprise. These firms are not foreign multinationals. They are **native, wholly owned Irish firms.**	Unit 6

Industrial policy	A means of promoting business and employment in the economy. It is prepared in consultation with social partners, e.g. National Development Plan.	Unit 6
Industrial relations	This term is used to describe the relationship between the employers and employees in a workplace and refers to the history of disputes between them. We associate good industrial relations with high morale and productivity, and poor industrial relations with bitter disputes and strikes.	Unit 1
Inflation **Know the Consumer Price Index**	An economic variable. It is a sustained rise in the level of prices based on a basket of goods, based on the average family. **It was 1.1% in 2020.** It affects employees' purchasing power and a firm's competitiveness.	Unit 6
Innovation	A person looks for something original, which will not be in direct competition with other firms. The person wishes to create a barrier of uniqueness around their own product.	Unit 2
Insurable interest	The household or business must have a direct financial interest in the exposure unit. They must benefit by its existence and suffer by its loss, e.g. you may insure your home but not the house across the road.	Unit 4
Interest rates	The cost of borrowing. Rates depend on the demand and supply of money. In the Eurozone **(-0.5%)** they are set for all member states. Measured using a **percentage**.	Unit 6
International trade	Refers to all the business activities of countries as they exchange goods and services. Ireland is a small, open economy and international trade is hugely significant for the development of our economy.	Unit 7
Internet	A vast storehouse of information about a huge array of topics, which includes words, pictures, diagrams etc., at locations called websites. It is a network of networks. The worldwide web (www) is a subset of the internet and is a huge information source.	Unit 3
Intrapreneurship **Person inside the business and not the owner**	Means that a person acts like an entrepreneur **within** the confines of somebody else's business. The intrapreneur comes up with **new ideas, new products** and new services, or helps to improve existing goods and services. The intrapreneur does not risk their own money but risks their reputation and maybe their job. These people show initiative, spot gaps etc., but remain in the relative security of somebody else's business.	Unit 2
Investor	This person supplies the finance for the project after examining the business plan. This person expects an adequate return. E.g. in a company, the shareholder (investor) expects to receive a return called a dividend, which is a portion of the profits.	Unit 1

Job description	Describes the duties and responsibilities associated with an advertised job. It includes title, place of work, conditions of employment and details of reward.	Unit 4
Job production	A type of production whereby one unique, specific, expensive product is made. It uses highly skilled labour. No goods are kept in stock, e.g. a designer wedding dress	Unit 5
Leadership **Know the styles**	The ability to influence others and to direct them towards achieving goals. It allows a manager to have a positive impact on how others behave. The authority of the leader must be recognised by the group. The group must have a shared common objective.	Unit 3
Limited liability	A form of legal protection that benefits the shareholders in a company. It means that in the event of bankruptcy, a shareholder can only lose a maximum of what they invested, i.e. they lose the value of their shares but not their private assets.	Unit 5
Market research • **Primary** • **Secondary**	The gathering, recording and analysing of all the information involved in the transfer of the goods from the producer to the consumer. It reduces the risk of business failure.	Unit 5
Marketing mix	The use of **product, price, promotion and place** by a firm as a means of achieving its targets.	Unit 5
Mass production	A continuous production option. It is used to produce cheap goods in large quantities. Goods are kept in stock, e.g. biros.	Unit 5
Memorandum of Association **Used by designated activity companies**	This document governs a company's relationship with the general public. It contains the name, objectives, share capital details and details of directors.	Unit 6
Minutes	A brief written record of what was discussed at the previous meeting. Minutes are read out at the next meeting and voted upon by those present.	Unit 3
Motivation	Recognition of the factors which cause people to put real energy and drive into their work. Reward is essential but does not necessarily mean monetary payment. It is a management skill influenced by **Maslow's Hierarchy of Needs and McGregor's Theory X and Theory Y.**	Unit 3
Multiples	Chains of retail outlets which rent or buy space at prime retail locations throughout the country, e.g. Eason's. They buy centrally and in bulk, and benefit from cost savings in this way.	Unit 5

Negotiation	Both parties sit down together and **talk,** and each side puts forward their side of the argument. Successful negotiation means that a **compromise** can be reached, but if talks break down... (see Arbitration, Conciliation)	Unit 1
Net margin	Measures net profit as a percentage of sales. The formula is: $$\frac{\text{Net Profit x 100}}{\text{Sales}}$$ This measures **efficiency** and is an accurate measure of **profitability**, as expenses have been deducted in order to calculate net profit, e.g. wages, rent, advertising etc.	Unit 4
Net pay	The amount that the employee receives. It could be paid in cash or by cheque or by pay path. It is the amount after all deductions from gross pay have been made.	Unit 4
Networking	The use of all available business contacts to further one's business. A business gains more by sharing ideas and information than it loses by not keeping them secret. It recognises that working with other people is a far more effective means of survival and expansion.	Unit 2
Organisation structure	Refers to the arranging of the firm's resources in a way that allows it to successfully achieve its objectives. Modern structures are flatter, and the layers have been removed, e.g. matrix structure.	Unit 3
Own brands	E.g. **Tesco's Finest.** These are a 'private' range of brands produced for large-scale retailers in 'private' packaging, e.g. Sainsbury's Irish whiskey is produced by Cooley Distillery. Cheaper packaging is used.	Unit 5
P21	Also known as the **balancing statement.** It is used when claiming a tax rebate (refund). It shows what the employee PAID versus what the employee SHOULD have paid. This may show an underpayment or an overpayment.	Unit 4
Performance appraisal	A systematic approach towards measuring an employee's progress, contribution and effectiveness in the workplace over a given time period. It evaluates present performance and measures an employee's future potential. It can be used when choosing the most suitable candidate for promotion.	Unit 4
Personal selling	Usually applies to high quality, expensive items, e.g. industrial machines. A face-to-face meeting gives the salesperson the chance to present a case, persuade the buyer and clinch a deal. A strong presentation highlights the benefits of the product.	Unit 5

Planning **Know the types**	Setting goals for the organisation and choosing the best course of action to achieve them. It maps out a successful route to achieve targets, e.g. Virgin Media's strategic (long-term) plan is to gain more viewers, and the Guinness plan is to regain the 18 to 30-year-old market.	Unit 3
Privatisation	The transfer of ownership of **State bodies** from State hands into **private hands,** e.g. the partial sale of Aer Lingus. It reduces the State's involvement in commerce.	Unit 6
Proactive people	Enterprising people who adopt a go-ahead attitude are said to be proactive. These people are not afraid to take risks.	Unit 2
Producer	This person/party combines machinery and labour to transform raw materials into finished products for consumers. They provide raw materials for other producers and finished goods for consumers, e.g. McCain frozen foods.	Unit 1
Product lifecycle **Always label diagram fully**	Refers to the level of unit sales over a given time. Products vary, e.g. Guinness stout has a prolonged lifecycle, whereas in Japan, the Walkman has a three-month lifecycle.	Unit 5
Proposal form	The **application form** in insurance. It contains all relevant questions. The applicant must declare all material facts on this form, e.g. if a house has a thatched roof. **It is used to calculate the premium**.	Unit 4
Prototype development	A stage of new product development whereby the original of the species is put together in a form suitable for testing. The prototype must be suitable for full-scale production, so testing is carried out. This is **a mock-up of the product.**	Unit 5
Public limited company (PLC)	Quoted on the Stock Exchange, e.g. Kerry Group. It has a minimum of 7 shareholders and no maximum. Its shares are transferable. It must meet strict Stock Exchange standards on profit levels.	Unit 6
Public relations	Concerns a firm's relationship with the general public and the communication of its policies, ideals, products and services. Publicity is the unpaid mention of the firm in the media. It generates goodwill for the firm. It addresses any complaints made against the firm; it improves the firm's **image**.	Unit 5
Quality control	Eliminates rejects as early as possible in the production process. It reduces waste and satisfies more customers. It eliminates the causes of defects. The firm may acquire a '**quality mark**', i.e. an award for consistent excellence.	Unit 3
Questionnaire	A document used in primary market research to gather information. It asks a series of appropriate questions.	Unit 5

Reactive people	People who prefer to wait and see are said to be reactive. These people are risk avoiders.	Unit 2
Recruitment	The process in human resources management whereby the correct people are attracted to the firm. The firm wishes to attract flexible people with the necessary skills and personalities to fill the vacancy in a flexible firm.	Unit 4
Retailer	A type of business that specialises in a given trade, and is the direct link to the customer. They also provide worthwhile feedback to the producer, e.g. Smyths Toys Superstores.	Unit 5
Return on investment (ROI)	**Also known as Return on Capital Employed** (ROCE). Measures the overall profitability and **efficiency** of the firm. The formula is: $$\frac{\text{Net profit x 100}}{\text{Issued ordinary share capital + Reserves + Long-term debt}}$$ The answer, which is a percentage, should be at least 2%. This is the return that the owner would receive by placing the money in **a risk-free investment**, e.g. bank deposit a/c.	Unit 4
Risk management	Gathering as much information as possible about uncertain situations, and minimising these risks and eliminating them where possible, e.g. installing smoke alarms, carrying out market research. Once a **risk has been identified**, it can then be managed correctly. It is **a planned approach.**	Unit 2
Sales promotion **Gimmicks**	The use of attention-seeking methods to attract customers to he product or service. It is used in conjunction with normal advertising and the product usually receives short-term attention. The bonus or incentive offered is usually related to the product.	Unit 5
Selection	This area of human resources management comes immediately after recruitment. It **chooses the most suitable applicant from a pool of candidates** attracted at the recruitment stage. Interview is the most common technique used in Ireland.	Unit 4
Service industry	In this sector, nothing is produced but essential back-up is provided to other sectors. E.g. accounting, legal advice, information technology, distribution, and financial services.	Unit 1
Single market	A market without barriers and with harmonised rules and policies, e.g. Single European Market.	Unit 7
Sole trader	A person who owns and controls his/her own business, e.g. farmers, retailers, hairdressers, plumbers, carpenters. **They do not have limited liability**.	Unit 6

Span of control	The ideal number of subordinates under the instruction of a superior, as part of the delegation process. The ideal number is 7 subordinates per superior, **but it depends on the abilities of the employees, the nature of the employment and the abilities of the superior.**	Unit 3
Spreadsheet	A software application package which allows the preparation of budgets, accounts, payslips and breakeven analysis, e.g. Excel. It improves speed, accuracy and efficiency of work and improves decision-making in the firm. It eliminates the boredom of doing repetitive tasks. It allows sensitivity analysis, which allows us to change any figure at the push of a button. It improves the storage of accounts and improves their presentation.	Unit 4
State enterprise	The area of a State's involvement in commerce. The government has a social objective to provide essential services, e.g. free travel on Bus Éireann to people over the age of 66. Profit is not the main objective.	Unit 6
Stock control	A system to find the **optimum** level of stock. This involves keeping an emergency level called a **buffer stock**. The firm may use **EDI** (electronic data interchange), which improves efficiency. The firm might introduce a **'just in time'** system, whereby stocks arrive as closely as possible to the time of use. This releases cash for the daily running of the business.	Unit 3
SWOT analysis	Used at the pre-planning stage, it breaks the business down into four categories. It brings a structure to the planning process and improves the organising process. It looks at strengths and weaknesses (INTERNAL), and opportunities and threats (EXTERNAL).	Unit 2
Takeover	When one company takes a **majority stake** in another and **assumes complete control**, e.g. IAG and Aer Lingus.	Unit 5
Teamwork	Seen as an advanced form of delegative participation, whereby workers make key decisions. Employers are the main instigators of teamwork. It flattens the organisation structure and each team member has input into decision-making.	Unit 4
Terms of reference	Refers to the purpose for which a report has been commissioned by the person who wishes to avail of the findings of such a report, e.g. the Hanley report related specifically to medical staffing in Irish hospitals. The writer of a report should keep within the parameters of these terms to ensure that the report is accurate.	Unit 3
Time management	Carrying out tasks as efficiently as possible in the time available. It involves quantifying of tasks, delegation of tasks, strict monitoring, and great discipline from everyone.	Unit 2

Total quality management (TQM)	A state of mind; a way of doing business which means that an organisation continues to improve. It is a set of rules and practices for enhancing customer satisfaction by providing higher quality products and services in a rapidly changing world. It looks for **zero defects**.	Unit 4
Trading bloc	A group of countries with free trade between themselves and a common external tariff on countries outside the group, e.g. **the European Union.**	Unit 7
Transnational company	A company owned by its parent and with branches in at least 6 countries around the world, e.g. Dell. These companies move worldwide in search of cheap labour and cheap raw materials. **There are 1,550 in Ireland.**	Unit 7
Utmost good faith	The household or business must disclose all material facts. A material fact is a piece of information, which may cause the insurance company to accept or reject the application or to vary the premium charged, e.g. thatched roof on house, drunk driving conviction, heart problems.	Unit 4
Video conferencing	A system which allows a live link-up via satellite, which means that meetings can be held simultaneously but at different geographical locations. It is a virtual face-to-face meeting. It eliminates travel costs and time. Meetings can be held at short notice. Information can be exchanged. Proceedings are recorded.	Unit 3
Wholesaler	A firm that buys from various producers in bulk and sells in smaller quantities to the retailer. The wholesaler is often referred to as 'the middleman' and provides worthwhile feedback for manufacturers.	Unit 5
Working capital	The short-term funding for the day-to-day running of the organisation. The formula is: **Current Assets – Current Liabilities** All firms wish to have a positive cash flow.	Unit 4
Working capital management	The managing of a firm's cash on a daily basis. It means that the firm can meet all of its short-term debts when they fall due. It also manages stock, debtors, and creditors.	Unit 5
Working capital ratio (current ratio)	This ratio is used to measure a firm's liquidity. The formula is: $$\frac{\text{Current Assets}}{\text{Current Liabilities}}$$ Ideally, it **should be 2:1**, which means that for every euro that falls due in the short-term, the firm should have €2 to meet it.	Unit 4

SHORT ANSWER QUESTIONS (SAQs)

This section is worth 20% of the exam and it is important that you know all the terms from the exam questions. It is better to write as much information as possible, as one sentence definitions are far from sufficient. There is a good mix of questions, varying from definitions to simple computations, to acronyms, to chart drawing.

It is wise to split all definitions into 2 separate points.

The more difficult past SAQs with model answers:

2019

> *Q.* Explain the term **national minimum wage.**

The **legal** minimum hourly payment to an employee, set by government. It is currently €10.10 per hour.

> *Q.* Describe **one** possible economic impact on **Irish business** of the increase in the national minimum wage.

Increased costs may result in redundancies. The increased hourly rate of hiring employees may force the business to reduce staff numbers.

2018

> *Q.* Outline two implications for a business of changing from a functional to a **matrix organisation structure**.

Training: Training costs are involved for managers and staff, and training takes time to complete. Staff development may result, as employees have greater knowledge and learn how the whole business operates.

Duplication of duties may exist across several teams: Several teams may have a marketing manager, production manager, etc. It is essential that each of these managers communicate to avoid conflicting approaches to projects.

> *Q.* Explain the term **working capital**.

The level of cash available for **the day-to-day running of a business**. It is used to pay current liabilities such as creditors, bank overdraft, accruals. **Working capital is calculated by subtracting current liabilities from current assets.**

> *Q.* Outline two problems caused by **insufficient working capital** for a start-up business.

It directly affects the liquidity position of the business. There will be a cash flow problem; this may make it more difficult to acquire loans.

The objectives of the business cannot be achieved. Short-term needs, such as the purchase of stock and payment of wages, cannot be met.

> *Q.* Outline your understanding of the terms **privatisation** and **deregulation**.

Privatisation occurs when a **State-owned business** is sold to **private investors**. Deregulation is the **removal of legal barriers** to allow firms to **enter an industry** or a market, or to trade in a market.

2017

> *Q.* Outline two factors that could reduce **bad debts** in a business.

Assess credit history: The credit worthiness of potential customers is checked in advance, e.g. asking for bank references, trade references, Credit Bureau, *Stubbs Gazette*.

Credit limits: Set appropriate credit limits and credit periods. Draw up clear terms and conditions controlling the amount of credit and ensuring that payments are made on time.

APPLIED BUSINESS QUESTIONS (ABQs)

→ Compulsory section

→ **80 marks (20%)**

→ **In Leaving Cert 2020, students will be examined on Units 2, 3 and 4**

Unit 2

- Enterprise
- Enterprise Characteristics
- Enterprise Skills
- Intrapreneurship
- Application of enterprise in the Home, School, Community, Government departments and Business Start-Up

Unit 3

- Management Characteristics
- Management Skills (Leading, Communicating, Motivating)
- Management Activities (Planning, Organising, Controlling)
- Management v. Enterprise

Unit 4

- Understand the central role of human resources in management
- Identify the strategies for managing change
- Discuss the importance of total quality management
- Understand the importance of accounts and business data in the monitoring of the business enterprise

In Leaving Cert 2020, students should note the following:

The student must know at least 8 enterprise characteristics and at least 8 enterprise skills, as this makes it much easier when relating to the text and gives the student a wider range of options.

A common mistake amongst previous Leaving Cert answers was confusing 'Management Skills' with 'Management Activities'. No marks were awarded.

Expect to be asked to 'evaluate' management <u>skills</u> or management <u>activities</u> from the passage.

- Define the skill or activity;
- Give a brief explanation of the <u>skill</u> or <u>activity</u>;
- Analyse it at present in the text;
- Offer methods of improvement and relate to the text

N.B.:

- There are three questions based on a given passage
- Students should read the three questions and note the allocation of marks before reading the text (a 40-mark question should be answered within 18 minutes)
- You must state your point, expand the point, and relate it to the text
- DO NOT MIX UP ENTERPRISE TERMS WITH MANAGEMENT SKILLS OR ACTIVITIES
- THE MATERIAL IN THE PASSAGE DICTATES WHICH ENTREPRENEURIAL WORDS ARE NEEDED
- **ALWAYS REFER TO THE PASSAGE**

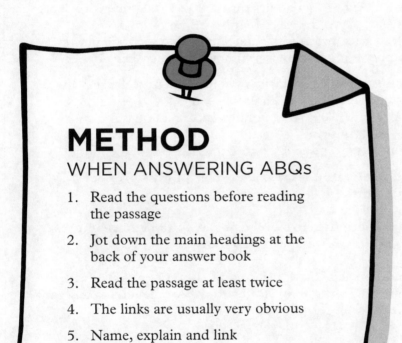

METHOD
WHEN ANSWERING ABQs

1. Read the questions before reading the passage

2. Jot down the main headings at the back of your answer book

3. Read the passage at least twice

4. The links are usually very obvious

5. Name, explain and link

6. You can use the same link in separate questions A and B and C, if relevant

7. If 'discuss' is the outcome verb, write mini paragraphs

 N.B.:

- **There will be regular updates on my website and lots of new ABQs for LCHL 2022 onwards:**

www.leavingcertbusiness.com

Sample Question for 2020

Mr. Stuffing

Andrew had worked in a multinational food ingredients company for 10 years in his hometown in the west of Ireland. He worked in the new product innovation section and was always on the lookout for a new and original idea. Three years ago, he spotted a gap in the market for food stuffing and ready-made sandwich fillings. As he had researched the idea at work, he felt obliged to point out the idea to his superior. She said that he was paid to research products that have global appeal and not traditional Irish recipes.

A year later, a disgruntled Andrew accepted a voluntary redundancy package and left the firm. He used his redundancy money to help to set up his own firm, 'Mr. Stuffing' and initially targeted the Irish market. He planned to create a high-quality product using natural and wholesome ingredients. He targeted a sales turnover of €500,000 in year one. He recruited staff locally and encourages teamwork, rewards staff innovation and encourages employee input at all stages. Employees are encouraged to focus on new ideas, the customers' needs and wants, and to minimise costs without ever sacrificing quality.

Mr. Stuffing is now one of the fastest-growing specialty food manufacturers in the country. Andrew now feels the need for a full-time financial controller to help to cope with the growth and to develop a strategic plan. The newly appointed accountant has informed Andrew that on first impressions the firm seems to be efficient, liquid and has scope for future borrowings. The accountant has promised a full report at the end of the month.

(A)   **Illustrate from the above information two examples of intrapreneurship in the above passage. (*20 marks*)**

(B)   **Analyse the management activities used by Andrew in the running of his business. Refer to the text in your answer. (*20 marks*)**

(C)   **Draft a report that would be sent by the financial controller to Andrew analysing the state of affairs in the firm. Refer to three relevant ratios in your answer. (*40 marks*)**

Part A

- This question deals with concept of 'Intrapreneurship' from Unit 2 and being able to recognise two instances of it in the passage.
- The student should focus on Andrew's discovery in the first paragraph and also his encouragement of 'teamwork and innovation' in the second paragraph.

Part B

- Deals specifically with the management activities of:
  (i) Planning   (ii) Organising   (iii) Controlling
- A comprehensive definition of each is important and the student should be able to relate to the text and point out examples of all three activities.

Part C

- This question examines a report which means that a specific structure is needed. It also examines the three key areas when monitoring a business:

  (i) Profitability   (ii) Liquidity   (iii) Capital structure

(A)   Illustrate from the above information two examples of intrapreneurship in the above passage (20 marks)

Intrapreneurship means that a person acts like an entrepreneur within the confines of somebody else's business. The intrapreneur comes up with new ideas new products and new services or helps to improve existing goods and services. The intrapreneur does not risk their own money but risks their reputation and maybe their job. These people show initiative, spot gaps etc., but remain in the relative security of somebody else's business.

Andrew "*spotted a gap in the market for food stuffing and readymade sandwich fillings*".

Later, we are told about Andrew's approach to his employees. "*He encourages teamwork, rewards staff innovation and encourages employee input at all stages.*"

(B)   Analyse the management activities used by Andrew in the running of his business. Refer to the text in your answer. (20 marks)

Planning is setting targets for the organisation and choosing the best course of action to achieve them. A firm maps out a successful route to achieve its targets.

Andrew wishes to satisfy customer needs and sustain profitability. Firms would have specific objectives and a range of plans to achieve them. The main plans are:

- Strategic (long-term)
- Tactical (short-term)
- Contingency (emergency)

"*He planned to create a high-quality product using natural and wholesome ingredients. He targeted a sales turnover of €500,000 in year one.*"

"*Andrew now feels the need for a full-time financial controller to help to cope with the growth and to develop a strategic plan.*"

Organising is an agreed means of using resources so as best to achieve our objectives? Traditional firms used a chain of command based on the army, with several layers, but modern firms have delayered the system into project teams on an equal footing. It helps a firm to achieve its objectives and helps to improve quality and staff morale.

"*He recruited staff locally and encourages teamwork, rewards staff innovation and encourages employee input at all stages. Employees are encouraged to focus on new ideas.*"

Andrew uses the modern style of working with the employees and encouraging teamwork.

Controlling is comparing the results with the original plans and measuring performance. The firm must take corrective action to deal with deviations which are affecting objectives. It helps a firm to achieve its objectives.

We are told that "*the employees focus on the customers' needs and wants, and minimise costs without ever sacrificing quality*". This suggests that Andrew has implemented quality control and cost control in his successful business. "*Mr Stuffing is now one of the fastest-growing specialty food manufacturers.*"

In the area of cost control, "*he has appointed a financial controller*".

– continued overleaf

(C)   **Draft a report that would be sent by the financial controller to Andrew analysing the state of affairs in the firm. Refer to three relevant ratios in your answer. (*40 marks*)**

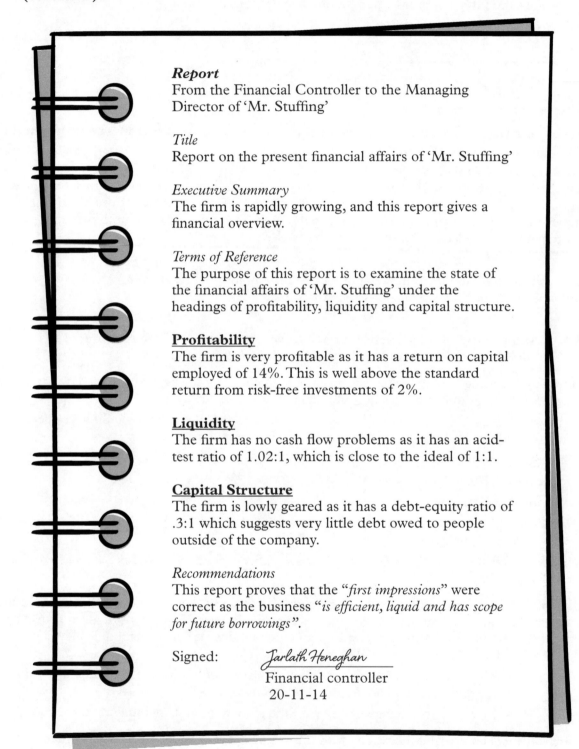

Report
From the Financial Controller to the Managing Director of 'Mr. Stuffing'

Title
Report on the present financial affairs of 'Mr. Stuffing'

Executive Summary
The firm is rapidly growing, and this report gives a financial overview.

Terms of Reference
The purpose of this report is to examine the state of the financial affairs of 'Mr. Stuffing' under the headings of profitability, liquidity and capital structure.

Profitability
The firm is very profitable as it has a return on capital employed of 14%. This is well above the standard return from risk-free investments of 2%.

Liquidity
The firm has no cash flow problems as it has an acid-test ratio of 1.02:1, which is close to the ideal of 1:1.

Capital Structure
The firm is lowly geared as it has a debt-equity ratio of .3:1 which suggests very little debt owed to people outside of the company.

Recommendations
This report proves that the "*first impressions*" were correct as the business "*is efficient, liquid and has scope for future borrowings*".

Signed: *Jarlath Heneghan*
                 Financial controller
                 20-11-14

Sample Question for 2020

Crispy Fresh Ltd.

Martin set up his own bakery in 1994. He had worked in the catering industry for several years but liked the idea of being in charge of his own future. He worked long hours and the business grew quickly. He recognised the need to hire staff and it now has 45 full-time employees. He always carries out research to help his business and believes in tackling problems as soon as they arise.

Recently, staff have made clear their dissatisfaction with Martin's leadership style. He has taken to giving orders and refuses to recognise staff grievances. The quality is suffering due to obsolete production techniques, but Martin finds it difficult to implement change.

His business advisor Maura has suggested that the bakery needs to replace all of its existing equipment at a cost of €100,000. Furthermore, the workforce needs to be trimmed to 20 full-time staff as the market has become increasingly competitive. The redundancies are vital to safeguard the future of the bakery. Maura is concerned with Martin's approach to making the necessary changes in the firm.

(A)   **Illustrate from the above information four enterprise skills shown by Martin.** *(20 marks)*

(B)   **Define leadership. Analyse Martin's leadership style and its impact on the business. Use relevant examples from the text.** *(20 marks)*

(C)   **Outline the strategies that Martin should use to implement the changeover to the new equipment. Using the information available about Crispy Fresh Ltd., explain your answer fully.** *(40 marks)*

Answer Plan

This question and suggested solution widen our revision to include leadership styles and the 'strategies to implement change' section from 'Changing Role of Management'.

Part A
• We are looking for enterprise skills and the question specifies that four are needed.

Part B
• We are asked to analyse the leadership style, so we should recognise the relevant style and be able to relate the answer to the text.

Part C
• One of the most important areas in Unit 4 is examined – strategies to implement change. When the question was last asked, the student had to expand three points and relate them to the text to gain 30 marks. For 40 marks, we would be expected to explain four points clearly and relate them to the passage.

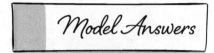

**(A)   Illustrate from the above information four enterprise skills shown by Martin.
(20 marks)**

Martin has displayed the following enterprise skills:

- Inner control:

  This means being in charge of your own destiny, being in control of your own future. It is
  driven by personal pride and determination.

  "*He liked the idea of being in charge of his own future.*"

- Risk management:

  This means gathering as much information as possible about uncertain situations, minimising
  these risks and eliminating them where possible e.g. carrying our market research.

  "*He always carries out research to help his business.*"

- Problem solving:

  This means that an entrepreneur knows the desired outcome and tackles problems in a logical
  manner. A proactive person sorts out the problem quickly.

  "*Martin tackles problems as soon as they arise.*"

- Delegating:

  This means sharing out the daily tasks to the subordinates. It allows the superior to concentrate
  on other areas.

  "*Martin quickly recognised the need for new staff.*" He had previously worked long hours.

**(B)   Define leadership. Analyse Martin's leadership style and its impact on the
business. Use relevant examples from the text. (20 marks)**

Leadership is the ability to influence others and to direct them towards achieving goals. It allows a
manager to have a positive impact on how others behave. The authority of the leader must be
recognised by the group. The group must have a shared common objective.

Martin has an autocratic style. This type of leader rules with an iron fist. This manager does not
trust the employees and does not recognise their abilities.

This style is having a negative impact, as we are told that the staff have made clear their
dissatisfaction with Martin's style.

He has also taken to giving orders and refuses to recognise staff grievances. This is bad for
employee morale and has a negative impact on productivity, quality levels and customer service.

**(C)   Outline the strategies that Martin should use to implement the changeover to the
new equipment. Using the information available about Crispy Fresh Ltd., explain
your answer fully.**

The following strategies should be used to successfully implement change:

- **Openness:** Consultation between Martin and his staff is essential through all stages of the
  change process. A more democratic and open leadership style would be more useful. He must
  make clear to the employees that change is essential as "*the marketplace has become increasingly
  competitive*".

- **Decision making:** Staff should be included in the decision-making process and workers' opinions are essential to future progress. Staff inclusion helps to implement the proposed changes. The economic benefits of change should be explained clearly to the employees of the firm. "*The redundancies are vital to safeguard the future of the bakery.*"

- **Training:** As the equipment is being replaced, the remaining staff should be prepared properly for the challenges which lie ahead. Staff will fear change until they understand the new systems and work practices. We are told that "*the bakery needs to replace all of its existing equipment*".

- **Patience and commitment:** It is important that Martin gives the project his full commitment. The most sensitive change concerns the redundancies and Martin should offer an attractive redundancy package to encourage staff to leave voluntarily. "*Maura is concerned about Martin's approach to making the necessary changes in the firm.*"

Sample Question 2021 – Units 3, 4 and 5

Hydro Clean Ltd.

Dan O'Brien had carefully built up his water filtering business. He planned for the short, medium and long-term. He regularly reviews his objectives and carries out a SWOT analysis twice yearly. His workforce is divided into teams and each team is allocated a specific project. Dan carefully monitors his production and eliminates defects as early as possible. He has introduced a just-in-time stock policy and this has improved cash flow.

Recently, he has noticed an increase in the number of claims made against the company. One of the company vans crashed into a parked car and an employee slipped on an uneven floor surface, injuring his back. A delivery man was injured by a falling pipe from an overhead shelf, and one of the firm's filters leaked chemicals into a water tank, causing substantial monetary damage to a customer. Dan is anxious that all insurance policies are in order.

Dan realises that to maintain a successful business he must diversify into a new and wider range of products. His research team consists of three environmental health graduates and he also relies on consumer feedback. He has read about brainstorming in a trade magazine and noticed some innovative ideas at a trade fair in London. He is willing to listen to all new ideas.

(A)   **Analyse the use of management activities in Hydro Clean Ltd. Refer to the above text in your response.** (*30 marks*)

(B)   **Outline the various types of insurance policies that Hydro Clean Ltd. should have in place. Refer to the above text in your answer.** (*25 marks*)

(C)   **Outline two internal and two external sources of new product ideas that Hydro Clean Ltd. could use to improve its product range. Refer to the above text in your answer.** (*25 marks*)

Solution

(A)   <u>Planning</u> is the setting out of specific goals and objectives for the business; it involves the putting in place of strategies that allow you to achieve the stated goals and objectives. Planning ensures that Hydro Clean considers its future and how it will achieve continued success. A *tactical* plan is a short-term one, e.g. an end to a strike.

A *contingency* plan is used to deal with emergencies, e.g. flood damage. *"He planned for the short, medium and long-term. He regularly reviews his objectives and carries out a SWOT analysis twice yearly."*

<u>Organising</u> is the management activity that usually follows after planning. And it involves the assignment of tasks, the grouping of tasks into departments, and the assignment of authority and allocation of resources across the organisation. *"His workforce is divided into teams and each team is allocated a specific project."*

<u>Controlling</u> is comparing the results with the original plans and measuring performance. The firm must take corrective action to deal with deviations, which are affecting objectives. The firm must:

• Set standards

• Compare actual results with plans

- Correct deviations
- Learn from mistakes

"He carefully monitors his production and eliminates defects as early as possible," shows that he has introduced quality control. *"He has introduced a just in time stock policy and this has improved cash flow,"* shows the effective use of stock control and cash control.

(B) The firm should have the following policies:

- **Motor insurance**

Hydro Clean Ltd. should have a minimum of third party, which covers damage to others caused by the firm's vehicles. Ideally the vehicles should be 'open driven' for all the firm's employees. This accident is definitely Hydro Clean's fault. *"One of the company vans crashed into a parked car."*

- **Employer liability**

This covers claims made against the firm by employees for work-related accidents caused by the firm's negligence. We are told that *"an employee slipped on an uneven floor surface and injured his back"*.

- **Public liability**

This covers the firm against claims by members of the general public due to accidents at the firm's premises, caused by the firm's negligence. We are told that *"a delivery man was injured by a falling pipe from an overhead shelf"*.

- **Product liability**

This covers the firm against claims by customers due to damage caused by our faulty products, which were not of merchantable quality. We are told that *"one of the firm's filters leaked chemicals into a water tank, causing substantial monetary damage to a customer"*.

(C) Hydro Clean Ltd. could use the following sources:

Internal

- **Brainstorming**

This means that Hydro Clean would use a cross-section of employees from the various departments and teams to hold meetings, with a view to developing and inventing new products. We are told that *"he has read about brainstorming in a trade magazine"*.

- **Research & Development**

A specialist team could use science and technology to look for new products, new uses for existing products or innovative production methods. We are told that *"his research team consists of three environmental health graduates"*.

External

- **Customers**

The closest external stakeholder is well placed to give an informed opinion on the need for new products as they are affected by all present products that attempt to satisfy their needs and wants. Customers are the best judges of what they need and want. We are told that *"he also relies on consumer feedback"*.

- **Foreign ideas**

Irish entrepreneurs are always keen to keep in touch with the industry outside of Ireland as many innovative ideas are developed in other countries. Similar ideas (without breaching copyright law) may work in an Irish context. We are told that *"he noticed some innovative ideas at a trade fair in London"*.

APPLIED BUSINESS QUESTION – LCHL 2021

Kate's Chocolates

In 1998, Kate spotted a gap in the market for quality handmade chocolates. She had worked for several years in a multinational in the Research and Development section.

Kate's team had specialised in sweets and confectionery, so the move to self-employed chocolate entrepreneur was something of a natural progression. She worked long hours initially to get the business off the ground and was usually the last to leave the factory each night.

Kate is well liked and tries to bring her staff along with her, rather than forcing them to follow. This approach works well, and the staff work hard in return. Kate wishes to grow the business year-on-year and the entire workforce put in the extra effort to reach pre-determined targets. The workforce is divided into 'product teams' and this allows the objectives to be achieved with minimum fuss.

Recently, her financial advisor John pointed out that while the business is profitable, it is going through a temporary cash flow problem. He blames this on Kate's tendency to hold large amounts of ingredients in the store area, and on her inability to collect outstanding monies from debtors on time. The latest set of financial results show a current ratio of 1.3:1 and an acid test ratio of .7:1. John has suggested that she tackles the liquidity problem immediately and Kate is determined to overcome the problem.

Kate is also looking to the future and is developing a new type of white chocolate. She is contemplating carrying out an extensive analysis of the Irish market but is off put by the costs involved. Nevertheless, she realises the importance of producing the right product to satisfy the discerning chocolate customer's needs and wants. This research would also provide valuable information on the correct price 'plateau' and enable the new product to be competitive. She has also heard that selling products directly to the consumer has certain advantages.

Kate knows that the confectionery industry is very competitive but is not sure of the specifics. The new product will also need to be promoted and Kate is unsure of the exact components of the promotional mix. Overall, she is leaning towards the market research idea and the notion that it would be money well spent.

(A)   **Outline the management characteristics that are evident in the above passage.** (*20 marks*)

(B)   **Analyse the liquidity situation in the above passage, referring to the current and acid test ratios in your answer. What solutions would you propose to help to ease the liquidity problems? Refer to the above text in your answer.** (*30 marks*)

(C)   **Explain the importance of market research for Kate's Chocolates. Refer to the above text in your answer.** (*30 marks*)

(A)   <u>**Characteristics of good managers**</u>

- **Self-Motivated**

Kate is driven by her own ambitions and an energetic approach sets a good example to subordinates. "*She worked long hours initially to get the business off the ground and was usually the last to leave the factory each night.*"

- **Achievers**

Kate has shown a willingness to succeed and has been able to set realistic targets and has had the desire to see them through. "*Kate wishes to grow the business year-on-year and the entire workforce put in the extra effort to reach pre-determined targets.*"

- **Charisma**

Kate has the ability to draw people towards her and subordinates are attracted to her style and work harder as a result. "*Kate is well liked and tries to bring her staff along with her rather than forcing them to follow. This approach works well, and the staff work hard in return.*"

- **Delegation**

A manager should not try to 'go it alone' and should share out the tasks where possible among the subordinates. Mistakes are tolerated as part of the normal learning process. Kate has learned to share the workload. "*The workforce is divided into 'product teams' and this allows the objectives to be achieved with minimum fuss.*"

- **Bias for Action**

Good managers are willing to try new ideas and experiments, and are prepared to have a go. They behave in a proactive manner and their 'actions speak louder than words'. "*John has suggested that she tackles the liquidity problem immediately and Kate is determined to overcome the problem.*"

(B)   <u>Liquidity</u> is a measure of the firm's ability to meet short-term debts as they fall due.

$$\text{Working Capital Ratio} = \frac{\textbf{Current Assets}}{\textbf{Current Liabilities}}$$

Ideally, this should be 2:1, which means that for every euro that falls due in the short-run, the business has €2 to meet it. "*The latest set of financial results show a current ratio of 1.3:1.*"

$$\text{Acid Test Ratio} = \frac{\textbf{Current Assets – Closing Stock}}{\textbf{Current Liabilities}}$$

Ideally, this should be 1:1, which means that for every euro that falls due in the short run the business has €1 to meet it. It is the true test of cash flow in a business. "*...an acid test ratio of 0.7:1. John has suggested that she tackles the liquidity problem immediately and Kate is determined to overcome the problem.*"

– continued overleaf

All businesses need cash to meet their daily spending requirements. It can be readily exchanged for goods and services, and adequate cash reserves means that the firm is liquid, i.e. able to meet short-term debts as they fall due. Firms are more likely to close down for cash flow reasons, i.e. unable to pay wages, creditors, or utility bills. A firm can make profits but must collect this revenue to ensure that it remains liquid, having a healthy cash flow.

This firm has a poor stock control policy and its cash is being spent on stocks of goods that are not needed in the immediate future. "*He blames this on Kate's tendency to hold large amounts of ingredients in the store area.*" The firm has a poor credit control policy and is unable to collect the outstanding monies owed to it. Debtors would be 'leaning' on its business and this drains its cash flow. "*…and on her inability to collect outstanding monies from debtors on time.*"

It could introduce a 'just in time' stock policy, whereby stocks arrive as closely as possible to the time of use, and this would release cash for other areas of the business. It could implement a more careful credit policy. It could get credit references on its debtors to minimise slow payments and bad debts.

(C)   Market research is the gathering, recording and analysis of all information involved in the transfer of the goods from the producer to the consumer. It reduces the risk of business failure. It is important because it collects and analyses information on:

(i)   Product

Information on consumer needs and wants gives the firm a better chance of satisfying them with the correct products. It will help to find a suitable package and name for the new product. "*Nevertheless she realizes the importance of producing the right product to satisfy the discerning chocolate customer's needs and wants.*"

(ii)   Price

Market research can estimate the parameters for price, e.g. between 50c and 70c for chocolate bars, and this ensures that her pricing systems are competitive. "*This research would also provide valuable information on the correct price 'plateau' and enable the new product to be competitive.*"

(iii)   Place

She can analyse information on place and choose a suitable channel of distribution for the products. Will she use wholesalers, retailers or direct selling to the customer? "*She has also heard that selling products directly to the consumer has certain advantages.*"

(iv)   Promotion

She can analyse information on the impact of the promotional mix; how successful is the combination of advertising, sales promotion, public relations, and personal selling. "*The new product will also need to be promoted and Kate is unsure of the exact components of the promotional mix.*"

(v)   Competition

Research will reveal the key players in the market. Any business wishing for a successful future should never ignore the competition and afford them appropriate respect. "*Kate knows that the confectionery industry is very competitive but is not sure of the specifics.*"

LONG QUESTIONS (60% of the exam)

There are seven long questions on the exam paper. You must answer four of them.

Part One
- Questions 1–3:
  Must do at **least ONE question**

Part Two
- Questions 4–7:
  Must do **at least TWO questions**

Fourth Question
- The **FINAL** question can be from **either section**

PAPER LAYOUT
AND YOUR ANSWER BOOK
- Label all questions clearly
- One part per page or pages
- Leave gaps between mini paragraphs
- Straight to the point
- No long-winded intro
- Name and explain
- Practise writing neatly against the clock

2021 COVID CHANGES TO HIGHER BUSINESS EXAM

→ **Written Examination:**
  - Answer eight from 12 questions.
  - No adjustment. However, in light of the choice introduced within the examination, the SEC will be cognisant of the word count of the ABQ.

→ **Part 1 and Part 2:**
  - Increased choice with four questions in each (i.e. one additional question in Part 1).
  - Candidates must answer one question from Part 1 and one question from Part 2, and any other two questions.

– continued overleaf

→ Watch out for the following outcome verbs, as they influence the marking scheme:

Evaluate

- In my opinion or judgement
- Two sentences explaining your opinion

Discuss

- Explain and explain
- Use mini paragraphs
- DO NOT USE HEADINGS

Know what *evaluate* and *discuss* mean.

→ **How to read an exam question:**

For example: *Evaluate how the Sale of Goods and Supply of Services Act helps to protect the consumer.*

There are effectively three parts to watch out for:

- Evaluate...
- SOGSOS Act...
- Protect the consumer...

See table for sectional guide to the minimum average mark's requirement for each Higher band:

	SAQs	ABQ	Q1	Q2	Q3	Q4	Q5	Q6/7
H1	72	72	54	54	54	54	54	54
H2	64	64	48	48	48	48	48	48
H3	56	56	42	42	42	42	42	42
H4	48	48	36	36	36	36	36	36
H5	40	40	30	30	30	30	30	30
H6	32	32	24	24	24	24	24	24

UNIT

1

Notes

Unit 1

Question 1 from the paper

> **(A)** Outline, using examples, the relationship that can exist between 'Investors' and 'Entrepreneurs' in business. (*15 marks*)

Entrepreneur
- This person is the promoter of the business who combines the factors of production into a business unit
- She/he takes moderate risks and takes the initiative after spotting a gap in the market and encounters success or failure
- She/he is the ideas person

Investor
- Supplies the finance for the project after examining the business plan
- Expects an adequate return; shareholders are investors and their return is called a dividend
- Money on deposit in a bank is the least risky but provides the smallest return

A *co-operative relationship* exists where joint action or effort is required to enable people to work and operate together so that all parties will benefit. This is a winner-winner relationship.

Example: The entrepreneur has a good business plan and the investor is happy to advance funds.

A *competitive relationship* exists when people inside and outside the business have common areas of competition and are competing against each other. They compete on a basis of price quality and labour. This is a winner-loser relationship.

Example: The investor refuses to fund the project.

> Explain how consumers may benefit from the existence of a competitive relationship between producers. (*15 marks*)

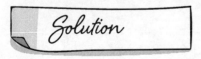

A competitive relationship exists when people inside and outside the business have common areas of competition and are competing against each other, e.g. **Coca-Cola v Pepsi**.

They compete on a basis of price, quality and labour; this is a winner-loser relationship. A relationship can be competitive and co-operative in an everchanging business world.

– continued overleaf

Price

Consumers benefit from lower prices as producers attempt to gain market share by competing on a basis of price.

Quality

Standards of quality are improved due to the existence of competition and this benefits the customers who get more for less.

EXAM WATCH

In more recent years, **DISCUSS** means **EXPLAIN** and **EXPLAIN**.

Illustrate the role of interest groups in business. (*10 marks*)

Solution

An interest group is a representative organisation outside of the political system, which puts pressure on other bodies to achieve an aim. This pressure can take the form of demonstrations, bad publicity, letters, petitions, strikes etc. They attempt to influence policy decisions which affect their members, and are also called pressure groups.

Example: The Consumer Association of Ireland called on the Irish government to resist changes to the **airline refunds policy**, which involves passengers being offered vouchers in lieu of cash refunds.

Describe, using examples, one co-operative and one competitive relationship that may exist either between or within organisations. (*20 marks*)

Solution

A co-operative relationship is one where joint action or effort is required to enable people to work and operate together so that everybody will benefit. It is a **winner-winner relationship**. There is a **mutual benefit** to each party.

Example: An entrepreneur has a suitable idea and puts together a business plan to persuade an investor to advance funds. The entrepreneur makes a tidy profit and pays a good return to the investor. Both are happy.

A competitive relationship means that the parties are on different sides or have conflicting or are directly competing with each other. This is a win-lose situation.

Example: A chemical producer dumps its effluent into the Irish Sea as this is the cheapest method of disposal. The interest group Friends of the Earth stage a protest to highlight the damage caused to the environment and consumers boycott the producer's chemicals.

Outline three remedies for breach of contract. (*20 marks*)

1. **Damages**

   Monetary compensation is awarded to the injured party. A court decides on an adequate figure.

   Example: The singer Robbie Williams sacked his manager and a judge awarded £1.7m sterling damages to the manager, who had honoured the terms of the contract.

2. **Specific performance**

   A judge **orders that certain duties are carried out**. It is a suitable means if damages are not appropriate.

   Example: A building contractor and a client disagreed over the quality of workmanship on a partially completed house. A judge ruled that the building contractor should upgrade the work and complete the house.

3. **Rescind the contract**

   A judge attempts to place both parties back in the same position as they were before the contract began. The purpose is to release the parties from the contract.

   Example: Assume you agreed to sell, and the buyer agreed to buy three acres of land that you thought you owned. Later, it turns out that you did not have title to the property. Rescinding the contract would be the proper remedy.

Evaluate the role of each of the following in protecting consumers:
- **Small Claims Procedure**
- **Government ombudsman**

(*20 marks*)

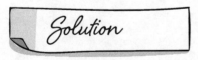

- Now called the Small Claims Procedure, it is a speedy way to access the district court system for matters not involving large values of money, as the limit is **€2,000**

- The civil claims are processed by a clerk of the district court called the **Small Claims Registrar**

- **EVALUATION:** It is a fast procedure with minimum red tape, a fee of only **€25** and no need for a solicitor

– continued overleaf

- An ombudsman investigates complaints from members of the public who feel they have been unfairly treated by certain organisations, e.g. government departments.

- His/her office is impartial and independent. If he/she finds a complaint is justified, he/she will take steps to secure redress for the complainant.

- **EVALUATION:** In my opinion, it helps ordinary citizens to get fair play when dealing with bureaucratic civil servants and puts pressure on government employees by making them accountable for their actions.

Outline the main functions of the Competition and Consumer Protection Commission under the Consumer Protection Act 2007. (*20 marks*)

The main roles/functions of the CCPC are:

- <u>To promote and protect the interests and welfare of consumers.</u> To inform consumers of their rights and/by providing a consumer phone service/website.

- <u>To enforce the relevant consumer law.</u> Enforcement tools include prohibition notices, undertakings from traders, compliance notices, on-the-spot fines for offences relating to price display, and the ability to 'name and shame' with the publication of noncompliant trader names.

- <u>To prohibit false pricing</u>, e.g. goods advertised as being reduced in a sale must have been on sale at the higher price for twenty-eight consecutive days (in a row) sometime in the last three months and at the same location.

EXAM WATCH

The underlined parts of the above answer are worth roughly half of the marks only. The remainder develops the answer and helps to achieve full marks.

- <u>To advise the government</u> of the impact of laws on consumers and make recommendations on legislation or policy, which concerns or is likely to impact on consumer protection and welfare.

Define employment discrimination under the Employment Equality Act and list five grounds for discrimination in the workplace. (*20 marks*)

The act defines employment discrimination as treating one person **in a less favourable way than another is being, has been, or would be treated in a comparable situation, and it affects:**

- Access to employment
- Conditions
- Training

Five grounds for discrimination:

- Age
- Disability
- Family status
- Marital status
- Sexual orientation

EXAM WATCH

The exact definition in law is needed for 'employment discrimination'.

The purpose of the Industrial Relations Act, 1990 is to put in place an improved framework for the conduct of industrial relations and for the resolution of trade disputes.

Outline the impact on trade unions of the main provisions of the Industrial Relations Act, 1990. (*20 marks*)

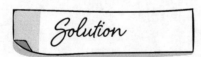

Trade unions are impacted as follows:

- **It specifies the grounds for a legitimate trade dispute**

  Dismissal: The sacking of an employee for an unfair reason is grounds for a legitimate trade dispute. This includes constructive dismissal.

  Employment policy: The firm could recruit employees who are not qualified to do the job, and this could cause conflict with the existing employees. This gives rise to a legitimate trade dispute.

– continued overleaf

- **It outlines the specific procedure for going on strike**

  Employees must hold a '**secret ballot**' on strike action.

  If verdict is 'yes':

  - **One week's notice** must be given to the employer
  - The employer may not block the strike with a '**late night injunction**' (often held in a judge's home). It is sometimes called an 'ex parte' injunction as the employees or trade union officials are not present

- **It specifies the rules on primary picketing**

  Picketing means that the workers gather at the entrance to their workplace carrying placards to highlight the existence of an ongoing trade dispute. It places moral pressure on people conducting business with the firm. Primary picketing takes place at the workers' own workplace and should be conducted in a peaceful manner.

  - Peaceful picketing is allowed if proper strike procedure has been followed
  - Employees only should picket
  - Picketing is allowed at the employees' workplace and not their home

---

Define a <u>legitimate trade dispute</u> under the Industrial Relations Act and outline four legitimate reasons for a dispute. (*30 marks*)

A legitimate trade dispute meaning 'any dispute between employers and workers which relates to the employment or non-employment, or the terms or conditions of, or affecting the employment of, any person'.

Grounds for a legitimate trade dispute:

- <u>Dismissal</u>: The sacking of an employee for an unfair reason is grounds for a legitimate trade dispute. This includes constructive dismissal

EXAM WATCH

Need the definition of a 'legitimate trade dispute' **in full**.

- <u>Employment policy</u>: The firm could recruit employees who are not qualified to do the job, and this could cause conflict with the existing employees. This gives rise to a legitimate trade dispute.

- <u>Range of duties</u>: The employee should not be asked to perform tasks that are not in the work contract or to perform menial tasks in comparison to qualifications.

- <u>Pay and conditions of employment</u>: This is the most common reason and includes rates of pay, overtime, holidays and all the terms of an employment contract or a collective agreement.

Outline four reasons for a fair dismissal under the legislation.

- <u>Competence or Qualifications</u>: If the employee is not capable of doing the job or is not properly qualified to do so, then it is a 'fair dismissal'. The standards expected must have been explained clearly.

- <u>Redundancy</u>: If a person is being let go due to economic reasons, e.g. to reduce the wages bill to save the factory, it is a 'fair dismissal'. The employee must not be replaced afterwards.

- <u>Gross Misconduct</u>: If the employee is guilty of fighting, drunkenness, drug taking or stealing in the workplace, they can be instantly dismissed.

- <u>Capability</u>: This centres on issues like lateness absenteeism and persistent absence due to illness. This is the most difficult area to prove for the employer.

UNIT

2

Notes

Unit 2

Identify the personal characteristics normally associated with entrepreneurial businesspeople. (*20 marks*)

These are the special traits that a person possesses.

- **Confidence**

  They have a very positive self-image and look for solutions and not problems. They have great self-belief and usually good intelligence levels.

- **Flexibility**

  They can change at short notice and are adaptable in their approach. They are prepared to deviate from plans when necessary.

EXAM WATCH

In enterprise characteristics/ skills questions, avoid the use of management skills or activities.

- **Moderate risk taker**

  They would take calculated risks, which have been minimised. These would be financial and a person's reputation.

- **Decisive**

  They have an ability to act on the spot and a willingness to take responsibility for decisions. They are single minded in their approach.

Define intrapreneurship and outline methods that EducaPrint can use to encourage it. (*20 marks*)

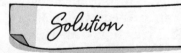

N.B.:
Very popular
with examiner

Intrapreneurship involves **entrepreneurial activity within** the business/employees come up with new ideas/take personal responsibility which may turn into profitable activities.

Intrapreneurs are inventive, creative, and innovative; they are constantly looking for ways of growing/expanding the business; and improving business processes/product, without the financial risk.

Methods of encouraging intrapreneurship, referencing the EducaPrint question:

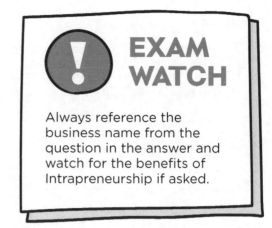

- Empowerment/employee participation encourages creativity as it allows employees greater freedom on how to do their job by placing real power, responsibility, and authority in the hands of employees.

- Financial rewards for effort and creativity. These rewards could involve a mixture of pay, incentives and benefits. For example, a bonus or profit-sharing scheme or share ownership scheme. John O'Leary could be given share options as a reward for his innovation.

- Teamwork encourages creativity among employees as it facilitates brainstorming sessions as part of the product development process. The matrix structure used by EducaPrint Ltd could encourage further intrapreneurship.

- Resource provider: Make resources available to help employees to pursue their ideas (e.g. finance, time).

- Training programme for employees and management: training them on the implementation of an intrapreneurial culture within a business.

Differentiate between enterprise and management. Illustrate your answer.
(**15 marks**)

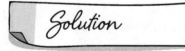

If the entrepreneur is the ideas person who spots the gap in the market and sets up the business, then the manager carries out the daily tasks by using the management activities of *planning, organising and controlling*. These tasks are performed by people and therefore the management skills of *leadership, communications and motivation* are used.

The entrepreneur is the risk taker who has shown the original initiative, whereby the manager also shows initiative (intrapreneurship) but a core element for a manager would be communicating with the various parties in a business (see Unit 1). In a small firm, the entrepreneur would also be the manager, whereas entrepreneurs like Michael Smurfit or Richard Branson employ managers to run daily operations while they dream up their next venture.

Define enterprise. (*10 marks*)

- Enterprise is being innovative and creative while taking personal/financial risk to achieve one's goal.
- Enterprise is when an individual (or a group of people) takes the initiative/starts something new.
- Enterprise involves the risk of organising all the resources necessary to provide a product or service while exploiting an opportunity for a possible reward called profit.

(i) What is meant by the term SWOT analysis?

- **Strengths, Weaknesses, Opportunities, Threats analysis**

It is used at the pre-planning stage and breaks the business down into four categories. It brings a structure to the planning process and improves the organising process.

(ii) Conduct a SWOT analysis on a business of your choice (include two points under each heading).

Name of business: Nivea

Strengths
- Nivea has strong brand recognition
- It has a strong financial base

Weaknesses
- Is the product still relevant?
- Is the market research up-to-date?

Opportunities
- New male skincare products
- To convert new customers to use current product

Threats

- New competition in the industry
- Consumers are more knowledgeable and expect more

EXAM WATCH

Strengths and weaknesses are internal issues, and opportunities and threats are external issues. It is wise to include two points under each stage.

UNIT

3

Notes

Unit 3

Describe leadership. Outline three leadership styles. (*25 marks*)

Leadership is the ability to influence others and to direct them towards achieving goals. It allows a manager to have a positive impact on how others behave. The authority of the leader must be recognised by the group. The group must have a shared common objective. The leader delegates tasks among the subordinates.

The main leadership styles are:

- **Autocratic**

  This type of leader prefers to rule with an 'iron fist'. Persuasion is using intimidation and fear tactics. This type of leader has no place in modern, educated workplaces. This manager does not trust the workforce and does not include them in the decision-making process.

  – **The result** is poor morale and an unhappy workforce.

- **Democratic**

  This leader brings the workforce along with them rather than forcing them to follow. Workers are trusted; therefore, work is delegated. Responsibility is shared and persuasion corresponds to the wishes of the majority of workers.

  – **The result** is a highly productive workplace with high morale.

- **Laissez-faire**

  This type of manager sets targets and then steps back and lets the worker get on with the work. The only interference is in extreme circumstances. Workers have a 'free reign' but this style only suits highly skilled jobs, e.g. computer programmers.

  – **The result** is a loosely managed but creative workforce.

EXAM WATCH

It is not wise to overlap points if contrasting autocratic and democratic styles as you may lose marks for repetition, and while autocratic leadership may exist in the army, the question will relate to a business.

Explain, using examples from a business, how each of Maslow's hierarchy of needs can be met. (*20 marks*)

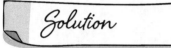

A business can meet Maslow's five needs in the following way:

- **Physiological needs**

  The firm should pay over and above the legal minimum wage to ensure that the worker can afford to pay for basic food and shelter for their dependents.

- **Safety needs**

  A firm should ensure that the worker feels safe from the fear of redundancy. The firm could offer a guarantee of employment to the staff, e.g. a letter of guarantee.

- **Social needs**

  The firm should provide time for social interaction both in the workplace and outside working hours, e.g. rotating seating arrangements in the work canteen and free meals after work on a Friday.

- **Esteem needs**

  Management should recognise an employee's efforts and praise them when necessary. The firm could promote staff as a reward for their efforts and offer them visible rewards, e.g. a bigger office. They should also be included during the decision-making process.

- **Self-actualisation**

  Management should recognise that workers are the best at what they do and have reached the pinnacle of their career. These employees should be encouraged to train and develop new staff and be rewarded for doing so.

EXAM WATCH

The stages must be named correctly and in the exact order.

Draft a memo from management to all staff in an enterprise, outlining to them a recently agreed method of staff reward. (*15 marks*)

Solution

MEMO

To: All Staff at Rapid Air

Date: 14/07/2019

From: Senior Management

Re.: Staff Reward

Please note that all staff will be entitled to a share of 10% of the firm's net profit for the year 2019.

Keep up the good work.

Signed: *Sean Booth*

Define span of control and outline the factors that affect a firm's span of control. (*15 marks*)

Solution

Span of control is the ideal number of employees that are under the supervision of a manager.

- **Skills of manager**
  The personality, skills and attitude of the manager will affect the span of control as some charismatic managers can handle larger groups, e.g.an unruly group of trainees would be suited to a narrow span of control.

- **<u>Type of work</u>**

  If it is a simple task and involves unskilled labour, then the span can be large but if it is complex with greater interaction needed, it should be narrow, e.g. straightforward factory machine work may lend itself to a wide span of control.

- **<u>Subordinates</u>**

  The education, commitment, experience and expertise of those being controlled will have a major bearing. Highly trained, motivated staff would be suited by a wide span but inexperienced, unmotivated staff would need a narrow span.

Use specific material here and watch for a wide and narrow span.

Discuss the statement that planning is the most important management activity'. Do you agree with this statement? Support your opinion with reasons and examples. (*20 marks*)

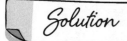

Solution

Yes, it is the most important activity.

Planning is setting objectives for the organisation and choosing the best course of action or strategy to achieve them. The firm maps out a successful route to achieve its targets, e.g. Coillte plans to quadruple timber production by the year 2030.

It improves co-ordination. It links all the various people in the organisation towards achieving the firm's goals. This helps to prevent the duplication of tasks and reduces levels of conflict.

It includes the views of all employees and plans have been agreed. It is the best method available of achieving objectives. As employees are included at the planning stage, they will stick to the plan.

'Discuss' answers require more detail and if asked to agree/disagree with the statement, use a yes or no, where appropriate.

It pinpoints underlying problems. As a plan maps out the firm's future, it forecasts future events and helps the firm to pinpoint problems, e.g. cashflow problems, stock shortages.

Examples:

A firm's **strategic plan** maps out its long-term future, e.g. Diageo, maker of Guinness stout, is targeting drinkers in the under-30 age brackets. The firm's marketing strategy has identified this section of the market as having the greatest potential.

A firm would have a **contingency plan** in the event of a power failure, and it would include the activation of backup generators. This reduces the chaos factor.

Outline the factors to be considered when choosing a correct form of communications. (*20 marks*)

- **Appropriate language (e.g. stakeholder, the consumer)**

If the language is too technical or too difficult for the customers to understand, then the message may be misinterpreted. The business needs to choose language appropriate to its audience. In the case of customers, short, clear sentences and visual supports etc. may be suitable for product assembly, e.g. flat packs.

- **Confidentiality (e.g. stakeholder, the employee)**

The medium chosen must be appropriate to the message being given. If the message is sensitive for the stakeholder, e.g. terminating the employment contract of an employee, then a meeting would be more appropriate than a letter or an email.

- **Cost (e.g. stakeholder, the manager)**

The expense of the communication process is a very important factor. A CEO communicating with his managers worldwide may choose to hold a virtual meeting to cut down on travel and subsistence costs.

- **Urgency (e.g. stakeholder, the supplier)**

If a crucial piece of information must be communicated instantly to a supplier, then a phonecall, a text or an email may be appropriate, e.g. to arrange a change in delivery times.

- **Feedback (e.g. stakeholder, the government)**

The business may be looking for feedback in order to take further action. Communication with the Revenue Commissioners may require regular correspondence and written records and, in this case, business letters and email can provide formal evidence of the feedback process, eliminating misunderstandings.

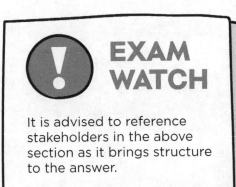

It is advised to reference stakeholders in the above section as it brings structure to the answer.

Outline the importance of good communication for the smooth running of a
business. (*20 marks*)

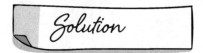

- **Clear instructions**

  Managers achieve work through people. Good communication is necessary when giving clear
  instructions to subordinates, to achieve the objective of providing a high quality good or service
  at minimum cost without sacrificing quality.

- **Employee morale**

  Good communication means that fewer labour days are lost, as there would be a good
  Industrial Relations climate in the firm. A good two-way communication process improves
  morale and reduces conflict in the workplace. Employee satisfaction usually improves customer
  satisfaction. This means that a manager has achieved his original objectives.

- **Suppliers**

  The firm will always have adequate supplies of raw materials if it maintains proper
  communications with suppliers. This means that delays are avoided, and finished goods are
  completed on time; therefore satisfying the consumers' needs and wants.

- **Customers**

  Clear information and a swift response improve the firm's relationship with the consumer. This
  improves the ability to satisfy their needs and wants. It also is essential in cases of conflict with
  the customer.

UNIT

4

Notes

Unit 4

> **Describe the three main short-term sources of finance used by a business.**
> (*20 marks*)

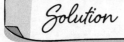

- **Bank overdraft**

  This is a facility offered by a bank that allows current account holders to withdraw more money from their account than they have in it. Interest is charged on the outstanding balance daily. It can be recalled by the bank at any time. The individual firm could use their overdraft facility to purchase stock or pay the wages of part time staff. It can be used as a form of working capital to aid in day-to-day business operations.

EXAM WATCH

Short-term sources for **less than one year** feature very often on the exam.

- **Trade credit (leaning on the trade)**

  Firms may buy stock for resale on a 'buy now and pay later' basis. The amount of credit available is influenced by the creditworthiness of the firm. There is no direct charge, but cash discounts may be forgone.

- **Accrued expenses (bills that are due or owing)**

  This source of finance frees up money by delaying the payment of regular bills such as utilities, rent or insurance. This would free up cash to pay for supplies which in turn could be sold allowing these bills to be paid later. There is the danger of disconnection of service in the event of missed payments.

> **Outline three sources of finance available to a householder for the acquisition of a car.** (*15 marks*)

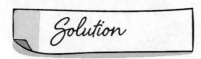

- **Hire purchase**
  - A person can obtain full use and 'quiet possession' of the goods by paying a deposit and a minimum of five instalments at regular intervals to the hire purchase company.
  - It is more expensive than a cash purchase, as interest is charged (as high as 20% Annual Percentage Rate).
  - Ownership passes only after the final instalment has been made.

- **Leasing**
  - Like hire purchase, in that the lessee obtains full use and quiet possession of the goods immediately.
  - No interest is charged but a lease payment is made at regular intervals.
  - Ownership will never pass between the owner and the user.

- **Medium-term bank loans**
  - The homeowner takes out a bank loan to cover the cost of the goods.
  - The capital sum + interest is repaid at regular intervals.
  - The homeowner may be asked for collateral against the loan, i.e. deeds of a house.
  - The person owns the goods and owes the bank.

Illustrate the usefulness of the debt equity ratio in helping a manager to monitor the financial performance of the business. (*20 marks*)

Solution

- The Debt Equity Ratio is used to measure a firm's long term financial make-up, i.e. its capital structure.

- 'Debt' is long-term debt provided by people outside of the business in return for annual interest plus full capital repayment on a specific date.

- 'Equity' is ordinary shares and retained earnings, and belongs to the owners of the business. They may receive dividends.

The ratio is:

$$\frac{\text{Long-term Debt}}{\text{Issued Ordinary Shares + Retained Earnings}}$$

- The relationship between debt and equity is also known as **gearing.**
  1. If debt exceeds equity, the firm is said to be **highly geared** and this means that large amounts of funds are used to pay interest. This reduces the firm's profits and its ability to pay a dividend to the ordinary shareholder (owners).
  2. If debt is less than equity (**lowly geared**) the firm knows that it can obtain further borrowings and profits are not eroded by interest repayments.

Examine the following figures from Savin Ltd.

	1997	1996
Current Assets	£ 91,500	£ 80,450
Current Liabilities	£ 62,400	£ 43,200
Closing Stock	£ 49,000	£ 40,100
Equity Share Capital	£ 250,000	£ 250,000
Long-term Debt	£ 253,000	£ 120,000
Retained Earnings	£ 20,000	£ 18,000

(i)   Calculate for 1997 and 1996:
   • The Working Capital Ratios
   • The Acid Test Ratios
   • The Debt Equity Ratios

(ii)   Applying your knowledge, comment on two trends that you notice
        developing in the business. Suggest what you would do about them.

(40 marks)

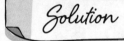

Working Capital Ratio = $\dfrac{\text{Current Assets}}{\text{Current Liabilities}}$

1997 = $\dfrac{91,500}{62,400}$ =   **1.47:1**

1996 = $\dfrac{80,450}{43,200}$ =   **1.86:1**

Acid Test = $\dfrac{\text{Current Assets – Closing Stock}}{\text{Current Liabilities}}$

1997 = $\dfrac{91,500 - 49,000}{62,400}$ =   **0.68:1**

1996 = $\dfrac{80,450 - 40,100}{43,200}$ =   **0.93:1**

– continued overleaf

Debt Equity Ratio $\quad=\quad$ $$\frac{\text{Long-term Debt}}{\text{Equity Share Capital and Retained Earnings}}$$

1997 $\quad=\quad$ $$\frac{253,000}{250,000 + 20,000} \quad = \quad \textbf{0.94:1}$$

1996 $\quad=\quad$ $$\frac{120,000}{250,000 + 18,000} \quad = \quad \textbf{0.45:1}$$

Comment:
- Liquidity has disimproved.
- W.C. ratio 1.86:1 to 1.47:1. This is well below the ideal of 2:1.
- A.T. ratio 0.93:1 to 0.68:1. This is well below the ideal of 1:1.
- The firm could introduce a Just-in-Time stock system to release cash. It could also introduce a stricter credit control policy.
- The gearing position has moved from a low position of 0.45:1 in 1996 to almost neutral 0.94:1 in 1997. This is because they received a long-term loan of £133,000 in 1997 (253,000 – 120,000). This means higher interest. The firm could issue more shares or plough back more profits into the company.

EXAM WATCH

Use the structure: **F**ormula, **F**igures, **A**nswer, **C**omment

LCHL 2000 Short Question Q7

	2000	1999
Long-term Loans	€310,000	€307,000
Ordinary Share Capital	€210,000	€150,000
Reserves	€98,000	€55,000
Overdrafts	€56,000	€76,500

Calculate the Debt:Equity ratio for each year and comment on the trend.
(***10 marks***)

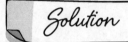

Debt:Equity

$$2000 = \frac{310}{210 + 98} = \textbf{1.006:1}$$

$$1999 = \frac{307}{150 + 55} = \textbf{1.5:1}$$

In 1999, the firm was highly geared but it moved to neutral gearing in 2000 (1:1). This means that the firm is funded equally by outsiders and owners. The change was caused by issuing more shares and by retaining more earnings.

EXAM WATCH

If commenting, mention the trend of the ratio improving etc, and a piece of accurate knowledge.

Outline the benefits of teamwork in an organisation. (***20 marks***)

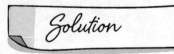

- Teamwork is an advanced form of participative delegation, which removes the layers in an organisation and organises the workers into small groups. It encourages intrapreneurship and problem-solving.

- *It improves decision making*
  A wide range of experience on the team means better decisions and teams come up with more creative and balanced solutions than individuals.

– continued overleaf

- *It improves motivation.*

  Workers are encouraged to think and participate in a constructive fashion and members see and appreciate each other's efforts.

- *There is a greater utilisation of talents.*

  As people work in small groups without rank or layers, they are encouraged to use all their skills and efforts. This improves morale and productivity.

Explain five different methods of reward for employees in a business organisation. *(15 marks)*

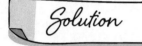

- Basic salary

  The employee receives a fixed monthly or weekly amount. It provides stability of earnings but may discourage motivation.

- Piece rate

  The employee's pay is linked to productivity, e.g. a blocklayer paid per block. It offers flexibility to the employee and serves as a good motivator.

- Bonus

  Exceptional performance is rewarded with a cash lump sum, e.g. a salesperson who passes their targets receives a €5,000 cash bonus.

- Benefit-in-kind (BIK)

  The employee's reward is in a non-cash or monetary form, e.g. use of a company car, free food, free accommodation, or staff discount. A BIK is said to be a financial reward if it is taxable.

- Profit sharing

  Employees receive an agreed portion of profits, divided between them. This discourages waste and absenteeism, and improves quality.

Contrast *'internal recruitment'* and *'external recruitment'* as a means of attracting suitable staff. (*20 marks*)

Internal Recruitment

- The employee is familiar with the culture, policies and work practices of the firm.
- Training and advertising costs are decreased. Motivation within the workplace improves as employees recognise that opportunities will occur as vacancies higher up the chain of command become available.
- *Example:* **Ryan Giggs** in his role as interim manager at Manchester United. He had spent his entire professional career at the club.

External Recruitment

- **Fresh new perspective** brought to the business by the external appointee.
- The new employee may have **skills and experience** that may be required by the business but are not present among existing staff.
- **Training costs avoided** as the external appointee may already have the skillset required.
- *Example:* **Jose Mourinho** had experience of seven other clubs before he was appointed to his role at Manchester United.

Define each of the following:
(i) Job description, (ii) Person specification, (iii) Panel interview. (*25 marks*)

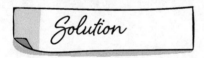

A **job description** is a realistic preview of the job to attract the right people. A job description sets out the purpose of a job, where the job fits into the organisation structure, the main accountabilities and responsibilities of the job and the key tasks to be performed. The job description defines where the job is positioned in the organisation structure and who reports to whom.

A **person specification** sets out the kind of qualifications, skills, experience, and personal attributes a successful candidate should possess. It refers to the person rather than the post and is useful in comparing and assessing the suitability of job applicants.

The **job interview** is used to determine whether the candidate and the job complement each other. A job interview is a process in which a potential employee is evaluated by an employer for prospective employment in the company. It is conducted using a range of prepared questions. Interviews generally take the form of interview panels **where several interviewers interview one candidate.** This series of **questions and answers** should be standard and without bias.

> **Illustrate how a good relationship between employer and employees can be developed.** (*20 marks*)

- Open Communications

  A good two-way communication system should always exist between management and staff. Meetings could be held to exchange information, including good and bad news about the firm.

- Grievance Procedure

  An agreed set of rules between employers and employees should be put in place as this helps to avoid conflict. These rules should be fair to both sides, fast to use and uncomplicated (simple).

- Valuing Employees

  Employees should be viewed as assets. They should be treated fairly and with respect. They should be offered better levels of pay, e.g. twice the minimum wage.

- Leadership Style

  Democratic-style leadership can be used, whereby the manager brings the staff along with them rather than forcing them to follow. Managers should be facilitators and not controllers.

  Example: A software solutions company, **Workday**, was ranked as Ireland's best large company to work for in 2019. Employee wellbeing is a major focus area for management.

> **Describe what is meant by performance appraisal of employees.** (*20 marks*)

This is a systematic approach towards assessing an employee's progress over a given time span in the firm. It helps all people in the firm to maximise their performance. It can be used to pinpoint training needs and takes the form of interviews, tests etc. It looks at previous targets and an employee's strengths and weaknesses.

Benefits:

- Provides information on staff

  It allows the human resources manager to identify high-performing staff and to recognise the difficulties faced by weaker staff, and identify a strategy to overcome these weaknesses.

- Motivates people

  The fact that people's progress is monitored and analysed means that they will constantly strive to improve and to reach those targets. They are aware that high performance will be rewarded.

Drawbacks:

- Cost

  Performance appraisal means lost labour hours and a series of tests and interviews that adds to the paperwork and bureaucracy in the organisation.

- Personality clashes

  Performance of the employee is usually done by an immediate superior, who may be influenced by the horns/halo effect on an individual employee. The appraisal will therefore be biased and lack objectivity.

> **Outline the uses of employee participation in an organisation.** (*20 marks*)

The uses of employee participation are:

- It improves quality for the customer

  The customer is the most important aspect of any business. Their satisfaction is the only lasting means of business success.

- The employee develops new skills

  Employees are given the chance 'to think' as well as 'to do', and are encouraged to fulfil their potential. This improves their productivity.

- Better decision making

  The employee is in touch at 'grassroots' level in the organisation and can pinpoint problems, and is encouraged to take initiative and develop new ideas (intrapreneurship).

- Better morale

  Employees taking part at management level boosts the morale and improves the Industrial Relations climate, resulting in a lower labour turnover.

> **Is the training and development of staff important for the success of the organisation? Illustrate your answer clearly.** (*20 marks*)

 Solution

Yes. Training prepares a worker for the challenges, which lie ahead and enables them to carry out the basic tasks for which they were recruited in the first place.

Induction training helps new staff to find their way in the business. It is the acquisition of basic skills and knowledge, which allows them to perform effectively.

Development is a wider process that enhances the worker's personality traits and growth in the organisation. It gives the worker confidence and familiarises them with the firm's corporate culture.

Staff development is focused on existing staff and enhancing their wellbeing in the firm.

They are both important because:

- They improve efficiency

  Workers know the job at hand and have the skills and knowledge to carry out tasks effectively. They will focus on quality, and waste will be minimised as they have been taught the basic skills.

- They improve motivation and morale

  Workers are happy in an environment where they are familiar with the workings of the job and the firm's ethos or corporate culture. Workers are confident enough to look for promotion.

> **Discuss the importance of TQM.** (*20 marks*)

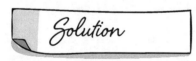 Solution

Total Quality Management (TQM) is a systematic approach whereby quality permeates the entire firm and includes all employees, all resources and all of the various departments.

It focuses on a customer-orientated approach and is based on continuous improvement, which ultimately satisfies more needs and wants of customers. Their satisfaction is the only lasting means of business success.

It reduces waste and associated costs as there will be fewer mistakes, fewer delays, and a better use of time. This also improves the firm's profits.

There is greater job satisfaction as empowerment, intrapreneurship and participatory decision-making are encouraged. Employees are faced with greater challenges and labour turnover is usually reduced.

Example: **Toyota** implemented the Kanban System to make its assembly line more efficient. The company decided to keep **just enough stocks** to fulfil customer orders as they were generated.

> **Discuss the changing role of a manager from controller to facilitator. Refer to areas such as the empowerment of workers and Total Quality Management in your explanation.** (*25 marks*)

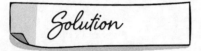

Modern managers are facilitators and use a democratic leadership style, whereas traditional managers were controllers and used an autocratic leadership style.

Modern managers have recognised that due to marked improvements in education, there is a greater need for consultation. Workers can now make a valid contribution (intrapreneurship) and new ideas are welcomed.

Modern managers are aware of the importance of delegation and its contribution to the decision-making process.

Empowerment is the transfer of real power to the employees. It allows him/her to work on their own, within agreed time limits and with agreed resources. Workers are encouraged to develop an entrepreneurial style within the firm.

Team-work is encouraged. Modern managers may lack the technical skills and are acutely aware of the need for a co-operative relationship with employees who have modern, high-tech skills. In many sectors, employees know more than managers and therefore, change was inevitable. Teamwork also improves productivity and morale in the organisation.

Total Quality Management is a state of mind; a way of doing business which means that the organisation continues to improve. It is a set of rules for enhancing customer satisfaction by providing higher quality products and services in a rapidly changing world. This is a customer-orientated approach and needs full co-operation from all employees to make it work. The change from controller to facilitator was therefore inevitable.

The growth of technology has transformed the way that workplaces operate. A change in management style was inevitable due to the growth of electronic mail and the introduction of teleworking, i.e. employees working from home. A facilitator type manager is much more suited to the implementation of new technology to improve production and enhance customer satisfaction.

EXAM WATCH

Note the extra detail for a higher order 'Discuss' outcome verb question.

Outline the strategies that could be used to successfully manage change in an organisation. (*15 marks*)

The strategies to successfully implement change are:

* Openness

 Consultation between management and staff is essential through all stages of the process. A meeting could be held, outlining the details in an open and honest fashion.

* Decision-making

 Staff should be included in the decision-making process and workers' opinions are essential to future progress. Staff inclusion helps to implement the proposed changes. The economic benefits of change should be explained clearly to all employees of the firm.

EXAM WATCH

Only use specific, prepared material as the question is not inviting you to make up strategies for implementing change.

* Training

 Staff should be prepared properly by the firm for the challenges which lie ahead. Staff will fear change until they understand the new systems and work practices.

* Patience and commitment

 It is important that management give the project their full commitment. Patience is imperative for all parties as all new projects have teething problems. All changes should be monitored and reviewed on a regular basis.

Define risk management and outline the strategies used by a business to reduce risk. (*20 marks*)

Risk management and insurance

Risk management is a **planned approach** to the handling of the risk that the individual or business is exposed to.

It involves:

* The **identification of all possible risks/losses,** e.g. the risk of fire, employer negligence, **personal** injury loss, legal liability etc

* **Calculating costs** of protection from loss

Strategies used to reduce risks:

- Insurance: Transfer the risk to an insurance company for a premium, where the company will make good any loss suffered.

- Safe procedures: The manner of doing something is strictly laid out and adhered to, and stringent monitoring procedures are in place.

- Health and safety: Health and safety statements should be in place and all staff should be familiar with the contents.

- Training of personnel in health and safety: Drills, courses of action and medical training all should feature prominently in company policy. Provision of safety equipment, protective clothing, and training in same. Health and safety representatives should be appointed in the workforce.

Audrey Stapleton is an employee at BAT Resources Ltd and earns a gross annual salary of €78,000. Her employer provides her with a holiday voucher worth €2,000. This is treated as a benefit-in-kind for tax purposes and is taxed accordingly.

The standard rate band for a single taxpayer is €32,800. (This means that the first €32,800 is taxed at the 20% standard tax rate, and the remainder is taxed at the higher tax rate of 41%.)

Audrey has the following tax credits: Single Person Tax Credit €1,650, PAYE Tax Credit €1,650, and Rent Tax Credit €320.

The Universal Social Charge (USC) rates on Audrey's gross income are 2% on the first €10,036, 4% on the next €5,980 and 7% on the balance of her gross income.

Audrey pays employee PRSI at 4% of her gross income.

(a) Calculate Audrey Stapleton's net monthly take-home pay. *(20 marks)*

EXAM WATCH

Show all workings in figures and in words. Watch for monthly, weekly or annual, and remember that the holiday voucher is taxable income but is not included in gross pay at the final calculation of net pay stage.

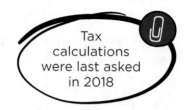

Tax calculations were last asked in 2018

Tax Computation for Audrey Stapleton

	€	€	€
Gross salary			78,000
Add benefit in kind			2,000
Gross income			80,000 **(2m)**
PAYE tax payable calculation			
€32,800 @ 20%		6,560 **(1m)**	
€47,200 @ 41% **(1m)**		19,352 **(1m)** OF	
Gross PAYE tax		25,912 **(1m)** OF	
Less tax credits			
Single person	1,650 **(1m)**		
PAYE	1,650 **(1m)**		
Rent	320 **(1m)**		
	3,620	(3,620)	
(A) Net tax payable		22,292 **(1m)** OF	
(B) Employee's PRSI			
€80,000 @ 4%		3,200 **(2m)**	
(C) Universal social charge (USC)			
€10,036 @ 2%	200.72 **(1m)**		
€5,980 @ 4%	239.20 **(1m)**		
Balance of €63,984 @ 7% **(1m)**	4,478.88 **(1m)** OF	4,918.80 **(1m)** OF	
Total statutory deductions			
(A+B+C)			(30,410.80)
Net income (take-home pay) p.a.			
(€78,000 – €30,410.80)			47,589.20
Net income (take-home pay) p.m.			
(47,589.20 ÷ 12) **(2m)**			3,965.77 **(1m)**

*OF = Own Figure

Define proposal form and outline three insurance principles. (*20 marks*)

Insurance proposal forms are used to **apply** for insurance cover, and the company is given full particulars of the risk against which the insurance protection is desired. Insurance proposal forms help the insurance company to **calculate the premium** based on all the potential risks in relation to the insurance policy.

- Indemnity

  This principle states that there will be no profit from insurance. The insurer attempts to put the insured back in the same position as they were before the accident occurred. E.g. if a second-hand car is stolen and destroyed, the owner does not get a brand new one.

  Exceptions:
  - Personal injury cases
  - Life assurance cover

- Subrogation

  If a third party is responsible for damaging your car in an accident and you are compensated by your own insurer, your insurer can then sue the other driver. Subrogation says when you accept an insurance settlement, the insurer gets your right to sue the third party. This prevents you collecting twice for the same damage and gives your insurer a way to recoup its losses. Fundamentally, the principle is linked to indemnity, ensuring that a person does not profit from insurance.

- Contribution

  This principle states that if you hold more than one insurer liable for your losses, they must share the loss. If you take out two policies on your car, you cannot collect from both insurers. One company would pay you and then collect from the second, or both companies would share the compensation payment between them. Fundamentally, the principle is linked to indemnity, ensuring that a person does not profit from insurance.

EXAM WATCH

Must know full definition of proposal form, and Average Clause **is not** an insurance principle.

Outline the factors to be considered when choosing a source of finance. *(20 marks)*

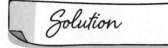

1. **Cost:** A business should try to obtain the cheapest source of finance available. The rate of interest is of great importance. All loans advertised by financial institutions should quote the **APR**. Close examination of the **APR** attached to each type of loan finance is needed when making the choice. A typical commercial mortgage in Ireland is 4%.

2. **Purpose/correct match:** Sources of finance must be matched with uses, e.g. a long-term business expansion plan should not be financed by a bank overdraft. Assets which are going to last a long time are paid for with long-term finance. Day-to-day expenses are financed or paid for with short-term finance. The firm should clearly distinguish between the three sources of finance and the timeframe for use and repayment.

EXAM WATCH

This topic appears in both the Finance chapter in Unit 4 and in the Getting Started chapter in Unit 5. This is important for ABQ purposes.

3. **Amount:** Large amounts of money are not available through some sources. Some sources of finance may not offer flexibility for smaller amounts.

4. **Control:** Issuing new voting shares in a company could lead to a change of power. The use of loan capital will not affect voting control but financial institutions such as banks may take control of fixed assets or impose conditions as part of the loan agreement. Recent acquisition at Kerry Group has diluted original farmer ownership stake.

Outline the purpose of preparing a cash flow forecast for a business. *(20 marks)*

A business prepares a cash flow forecast for a number of reasons:

* **Identify potential shortfalls in cash balances in advance** – think of the cash flow forecast as an 'early warning system'. A potential deficit is flagged at an early stage for the business.

* **Make sure that the business can afford to pay suppliers and employees.** Suppliers who do not get paid will soon stop supplying the business; it is even more damaging if employees are not paid on time.

* **Spot problems with customer payments** – preparing the forecast encourages the business to look at how quickly customers are paying their debts. Many businesses that do not offer credit terms do not have this problem, e.g. large supermarkets.

* **As an important discipline of financial planning** – the cash flow forecast is an important management process, similar to preparing business budgets.

Outline the reasons why households prepare cash flow forecasts. (*15 marks*)

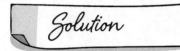 Solution

Reasons why households prepare cash flow forecasts:

1. It helps the household manage its cash flow and live within its means. It acts as a control mechanism that can be used to measure actual cash flow against planned cash flow, encouraging households to plan their finances sensibly and live within their means.

2. It helps a household identify periods of time in the future when the household will have an **excess of expenditure over income**, i.e. a deficit, and then take corrective action to deal with the cash shortfall.

3. It helps a household identify periods of time in the future when the household will have a **surplus of income over expenditure**. The household can then make plans to place these surplus funds on deposit with a financial institution.

Study the cash flow forecast below and fill in the figures represented by the letters A, B, C, D and E.

Cash flow forecast for Intenso Ltd, for the 3rd quarter of 2017				
	July (€)	**August (€)**	**September (€)**	**Total (€)**
Total Receipts	20,000	**A =**	12,000	57,000
Total Payments	14,000	17,000	15,000	46,000
Net Cash	6,000	8,000	**B =**	**C =**
Opening Cash	5,000	11,000	19,000	**D =**
Closing Cash	11,000	19,000	16,000	**D =**

 Solution

A = €25,000
B = (€3,000)
C = €11,000
D = €5,000
E = €16,000

> **Outline the limitations of ratios as a means of monitoring a business.** (*15 marks*)

Solution

- **Accounting policies**

  The firm must keep the same accounting methods and standards from year to year.

- **Seasonal factors**

  Factors such as unusual weather conditions can distort the true picture within the firm.

- **Industrial Relations climate**

  A set of figures might disguise the fact that there are bad relations between employers and employees.

- **Not comparing like with like**

  If we compare two firms that are in the same industry, the picture will be reasonably accurate.

UNIT

5

Notes

Unit 5

> **Outline the functions of a business plan.** (*20 marks*)

Solution

- It outlines the future direction of a business. It maps out the best course of action to achieve pre-agreed tasks.
- It shows evidence of research and highlights the capabilities of the project. It includes details about the product, key personnel, details of competition and a market overview.
- It provides projections of future trading expectations and cash flow, and demonstrates the business's repayment capacity for outside investors.
- It co-ordinates all the people within the organisation and directs them towards achieving tangible results. It acts as a useful guide or benchmark.
- It communicates important information to key staff and investors, both internally and externally.
- *Example:* The Irish Water business plan shows stakeholders that it intends to spend €326 million every year until 2021, on infrastructure upgrades.

> **Describe the main challenges to be considered when setting up a business.** (*25 marks*)

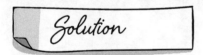

Solution

The factors to be considered when setting up a business:

- Product or Service: The firm must carry out research. The product or service should match the needs and wants of customers. It should look for a niche market supplying to exact customer requirements.
- Raising Finance/Capital: The business will have to choose suitable short-term (a bank overdraft to pay wages), medium-term (leasing equipment and machinery) and long-term (mortgage to purchase buildings) sources of finance. The business will have to raise finance to establish itself and survive. It will have to manage its cash flow and, in particular, its loan repayments.
- Ownership Option: The business will have to choose a suitable ownership option, e.g. sole trader, partnership or private limited company. A company may be attractive because it offers the benefit of **limited liability**. A partnership allows new skills to be acquired, whereas a sole trader may be attractive because the owners retain control.
- Production Method (manufacturing firm): The business must choose a suitable method of production, e.g. job, mass, or batch production. The method chosen must suit the business, guarantee quality, and ensure competitive prices.
- Recruitment: The business must recruit suitable staff with the right skills and qualifications, who will enable the business to achieve its objectives. Trying to find workers who can work in teams, have good communications skills and work ethic is a challenge associated with a business start-up.

> **Distinguish between the main production options available to a new business.** (*20 marks*)

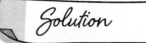

The main production options are:

Job production
- Usually exclusive and expensive goods are involved
- It involves producing custom work, such as a one-off product for a specific customer
- Production will incorporate the use of skilled labour
- There will be no stock of finished goods left over
- A level of automation is involved
- *Example:* Singer Mariah Carey wore a $25,000 Vera Wang-designed dress for her first wedding

Batch production
- Usually limited groups of identical, cheap product are made, e.g. tins of beans
- Each batch goes through one stage of the production process before moving onto next stage
- There is the use of skilled and unskilled labour
- There will be a stock of finished goods left over
- There is a level of automation and machines are flexible
- *Example*: Brennans Bread produces several different products in batches

Mass production
- There is usually a cheap product, e.g. pens
- Unskilled labour is usually used
- There will be a large stock of finished goods left over
- A high level of automation is used
- It is appropriate when firms are looking to produce a high volume of similar items
- *Example*: Car manufacturing

Distinguish between mergers and takeovers as methods of expansion. *(15 marks)*

Merger:

- A friendly or voluntary amalgamation or joining together of two or more firms for their mutual benefit, trading under a common name.
- A single new legal entity is formed once it is approved by shareholders.
- *Example:* Paddy Power betting company merged with the betting exchange Betfair to form Flutter Entertainment in 2015.

EXAM WATCH

Definitions must be thorough and precise in this chapter.

Takeover:

- **COMPLETE CONTROL**
- This occurs when one company purchases 51% or more of the shares in another company in either a hostile or friendly manner.
- The acquiring company absorbs the other company, which loses its identity after the acquisition and becomes part of the acquiring company.
- The cost of the takeover can be very expensive. *Example:* AbbVie's takeover of rival company Allergan in a deal worth €55 billion.

Contrast equity and loan capital as sources of finance for expansion. *(30 marks)*

The main differences are:

- Equity is supplied by the owner of the firm, whereas debt comes from people who are outside the firm.
- Equity consists of Issued Ordinary Shares and Retained Earnings (ploughed back profits), whereas debt consists of long-term loans.
- The providers of the equity for expansion would have a vote and could take part in decision-making, whereas providers of debt have no say in running the expanded business.
- The providers of equity may or may not receive a dividend depending on profitability, but outsiders must receive interest.

EXAM WATCH

Contrast means show the differences between something.

– continued overleaf

- Expansion using equity does not require collateral but expansion by debt will require collateral; usually deeds to the premises.

- Expansion by debt carries greater risk than the equity option – if the expanded business defaults on the loan (which is repayable) on a specific debt, the company may be closed down; whereas equity has no specific repayment date.

Example: The **Centreparcs** development in Co. Longford was partially funded by **€165m of debt** from a consortium of banks.

> **Evaluate the elements of the marketing mix using a product or service of your choice.** (*35 marks*)

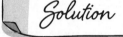

Name: Nike

Product:

The product is made up of the detailed characteristics, which the item has to offer. Its aim is to satisfy consumer's needs and wants but it must be produced profitably.

The product includes all the extra features. It includes design, packaging, branding, and the product lifecycle.

For example, the business continues its investment in research and development to produce new products and enhanced versions of its current products.

Price:

The price is extremely important as we attempt to satisfy consumers' needs and wants profitably. The price will attract or discourage customers, and some will be sensitive to price changes and others will take less notice.

Various factors and pricing strategies are considered by Nike. The premium pricing strategy involves high prices, based on a premium branding strategy that establishes Nike products as higher in quality and value than competing products.

Place (channels of distribution):

Although figures vary widely from product to product, roughly a fifth of the cost of a product goes on getting it to the customer. 'Place' is concerned with various methods of transporting and storing goods, and then making them available to the customer.

Getting the right product to the right place at the right time involves the distribution system. The choice of distribution method will depend on a variety of circumstances. It will be more convenient for some manufacturers to sell to wholesalers who then sell to retailers, while others will prefer to sell directly to retailers or customers.

The following places/venues form Nike's distribution strategy, arranged according to significance:

1. Retail stores
2. Nike online store
3. Niketown retail outlets (company-owned)

Retail stores are the most significant places where Nike products are sold because these venues are strategically located and easily accessible in various markets around the world.

Promotion

Promotion is the 4th P and is concerned with communicating with customers and potential customers. Its purpose is to inform the public that the firm has something available, which will exceed the customers' needs and wants.

It is an action taken by a company's marketing staff with the intention of encouraging the sale of a good or service to their target market.

It includes:

1. Advertising
2. Sales promotion (gimmicks)
3. Public relations and sponsorship
4. Personal selling

Advertising is one of the biggest contributors to Nike's ability to attract customers. The company heavily relies on advertisements, especially those that involve high-profile celebrity endorsers, such as professional athletes and sports teams. This element of the company's marketing mix also includes personal selling through sales personnel who persuade target consumers to buy the company's products. For example, sales personnel at Niketown retail outlets are trained to use such persuasion.

Evaluation:

In my opinion, the Nike marketing mix has been very successful, and the company reported annual sales revenue of $39 billion for the year 2019.

EXAM WATCH

Course knowledge of the marketing mix is more important than the examples in the above answer.

> **Evaluate three promotional methods for a product or service of your choice.**
> (*30 marks*)

Promotion is the 4th P and is concerned with communicating with customers and potential customers. Its purpose is to inform the public that the firm has something available, which will exceed the customers' needs and wants.

The main elements are:

Advertising

- Advertising is the communication of information about a product or service to the general public in the hope of selling the good or service.
- An advert attempts to:
  - Inform the general public about a product uses and characteristics. Persuade the customer that they need (usually non-essential) items.
  - Remind the customer that the product has not gone away and maintain a high profile.
  - Increase sales and profits.
- Ryanair runs a very successful 'in your face' advertising campaign. It targets customers everywhere, e.g. newspapers, TV, billboards. The adverts are difficult to escape.

Sales Promotion

- This is the use of attention-seeking methods to attract customers to the product or service used. It is used in conjunction with normal advertising and the product usually receives short-term attention. The bonus or incentive offered is usually related to the product.
- Examples of the **gimmicks** used:
  - Money off coupons
  - 25% extra
  - 6 for the price of 4
  - Tokens
  - Free gift with the product
  - Buy one get one free
  - Free samples
  - Games and scratch cards
- Ryanair offers free flights if you book before a certain date and regularly has massive sales of millions of cheap tickets.

Public Relations and Sponsorship

- PR concerns the firm's relationship with the general public and the communication of its policies, ideals, products and services.
- Publicity is the unpaid mention of the firm in the media.
- Public relations promotes the image of the firm in the public's mind and generates goodwill for the firm's products.
- Ryanair spends as little as possible on advertising. It sponsors major horse racing festivals and has a very active PR department.

Outline the uses of a breakeven chart. (*15 marks*)

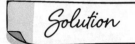 *Solution*

- It shows the point of production at which the firm makes no profit or loss, i.e. it has broken even, and total costs are equal to total revenues.
- It allows us to show the effects of an increase in our costs.
- It allows us to show the effects of a change in selling price.
- It shows the profit or loss made from a specific level of production.
- It shows our margin of safety, i.e. the number of units by which we can afford to reduce production before we start to make a loss.

Barton DAC supplies the following information about its activities:
- **Fixed costs €300,000**
- **Selling price per unit €30**
- **Variable cost per unit €15**
- **Forecast output 40,000 units**

Illustrate by means of a breakeven chart:
- **Breakeven point**
- **Margin of safety**
- **Profit at forecast output**

(*30 marks*)

 *Solution*

Preparing a table is useful as the figures will pick up marks even if the chart is incomplete

Units	FC	VC	TC	TR	P/L
0	€300,000	0	€300,000	0	(€300,000)
10,000	€300,000	€150,000	€450,000	€300,000	(€150,000)
20,000	€300,000	€300,000	€600,000	€600,000	BEP
30,000	€300,000	€450,000	€750,000	€900,000	€150,000
40,000	€300,000	€600,000	€900,000	€1,200,000	€300,000

– continued overleaf

We can use the breakeven formula to prove the answer:

$$\frac{\text{Fixed costs}}{\text{Selling price per unit} - \text{Variable cost per unit}} \qquad \frac{€300,000}{€30 - €15} \qquad = \textbf{20,000 units}$$

A breakeven chart is a series of three lines drawn on an x-axis and a y-axis.
The lines needed are:

- Fixed costs
- Total costs
- Total revenue

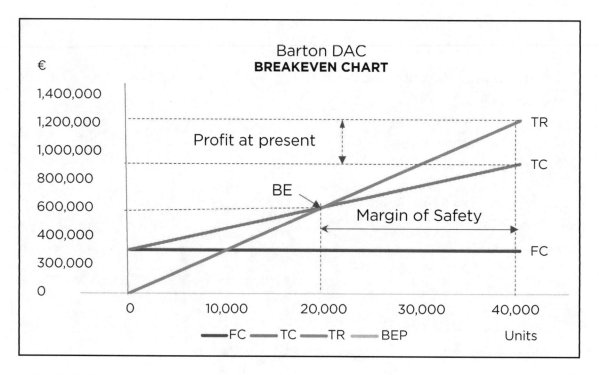

* *See inside back cover of this book for a colour version of this chart*

> Analyse the development process of a new product or service of your choice, under the following headings:
>
> **(i)   Idea generation**
>
> **(ii)   Product screening**
>
> **(iii) Concept development**
>
> **(iv)   Feasibility study**
>
> **(v)   Prototype development**
>
> *(40 marks)*

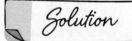

Product: PlayStation 4

(i)   Idea generation

This is the search for all possible products that could be offered to the consumer. Several ideas gathered should eventually lead to a few good ones. **Brainstorming** is often used. This means forming a think tank of employees from a cross-section of the firm. The session, which is often held 'off-site', must produce definite ideas before it is concluded.

EXAM WATCH

The stages must be in the correct order.

This is an efficient, methodical way of finding ideas for new products and services and can come from internal or external sources.

At this stage, Sony would have conducted environmental analysis, SWOT etc., to assess and predict the likely future of the gaming market and, more importantly, their position within it. This would have helped identify a competitive and distinct position for PS4.

(ii)   Product screening

At this stage they eliminated unsuitable ideas and concentrated on those with the greatest potential. Screening eliminates poor ideas as early as possible and concentrates on turning good ones into profitable ones.

This phase would have brought commercial and technical realities to the idea generation.

(iii) Concept development

This means that a product must be put together in a meaningful manner for consumers. It must satisfy consumer needs and wants and be in some way different.

A unique selling point is highlighted to distinguish the product from the rest.

– continued overleaf

For Sony, this phase would have been about establishing some key insights on the concept itself. So, does the consumer understand the product and is there a genuine need for it? Qualitative and quantitative research would have been conducted at this stage to ensure the consumer benefit is understood; feedback on the best way to market the product; and any weaknesses to understand and overcome.

Central to this was ensuring a genuine improvement from PS3 and that consumers will understand and value these improvements. It is about valued innovation and not innovation for the sake of it.

(iv)   Feasibility study

The firm looked at the impact of the product on the areas of costs, revenues, and profits. The demand for sales was forecasted and contribution and breakeven point were established. Can the product be made successfully?

The feasibility study takes place after the concept development phase and investigates how **viable** it will be to produce the product in terms of production, cost, and profitability. A feasibility study is an investigative report into the potential and profitability of a business idea.

- **(a) Market feasibility** i.e. is there a demand for the product; what is the best marketing mix for the product; and what are the sales figures likely to be?

- **(b) Financial feasibility** i.e. can the business finance the development, production and marketing of the product?

- **(c) Production/technical feasibility** i.e. does the business have the machinery, equipment and buildings to manufacture the product?

- **(d) Skills feasibility** i.e. does the business have the requisite skills to make the product, e.g. management skills and employee skills, or will training be required and if so, how much will this training cost?

- **(e) Environmental feasibility** i.e. will the production processes necessary for the new product have an impact on the local environment? Will planning permission be required?

The feasibility study would have been conducted after the launch of PS3 and looked at things such as:

- **Estimated production costs**

- **Gaming trends**

- **Broader technology trends (importance of mobile and social media, etc)**

(v)   Prototype development

Prototype development is the creation of the first working model/mock-up/sample of a new product/producing an update/improvement of an existing product?

This cycle is the only method for refining the original design to create a fully functioning product. It is a lengthy and expensive phase.

It is important to develop a prototype for test marketing.

A working prototype was produced, and beta tested with developers/gamers to identify issues with the proposed spec and to highlight necessary refinements and potential new features.

Many businesses spend large sums of money developing a 'brand name'. Illustrate the benefits of branding for the business and the consumer. (*25 marks*)

Benefits of branding to the business

- It provides instant recognition in the eyes of consumers, and a good brand achieves **'market standout'** and increases sales.
- It facilitates the **launch of a new product** as the consumer is familiar with the name already, e.g. consumers who were familiar with Calvin Klein Contradiction will know what to expect from CK Everyone.
- Brand names often make their way into the **English language**, e.g. biro (originally was a brand of ballpoint pen).

Benefit to consumers

- It creates an image for the product of **confidence and acceptability** and consumers become loyal to the product.
- Consumers associate brands with **superior quality** and brands are also associated with **consistency**. The consumer knows what to expect.

Example: Nike is a famous brand of sportswear

> **Within the product element of the marketing mix, evaluate 'product design' and 'product packaging'.** (*20 marks*)

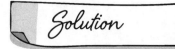

Product design

Function: This is linked into the main clauses of the Sale of Goods and Supply of Services Act 1980, which puts a legislative onus on producers to manufacture goods that are of merchantable quality and fit for the purpose intended. The product must do what it is expected to, e.g. a lawnmower should operate as expected and cut grass properly.

Form: The product must be aesthetically appealing in terms of shape, size, colour, style, image etc, e.g. iPad.

Evaluation

The value of this approach is that the specific needs of the consumer will be met, in line with the marketing concept. This will lead to repeat purchasing, consumer loyalty and ultimately, increased sales and profits for the business.

Packaging is an important marketing tool, as it remains with the product at point of purchase until the product is used. It also gives the product a good visual image and, through display techniques, distinguishes it from competing products.

A package should:

1. Be **<u>attractive</u>** in appearance and achieve market standout from rival brands. Many consumers judge the product by appearance.

2. Be **<u>practical</u>**: A package should ensure that the good is fit-for-use after going through the various channels of distribution.

3. Display **<u>legalities</u>**. It should contain details of ingredients, best before date, additives, etc. It show also show the trademark.

Packaging should offer:

• **Protection**: Packaging safeguards the product during transit, storage, and handling. It also keeps the product fresh, preserving quality until it is used.

• **Information:** The packaging contains information on contents, ingredients, best before date, health warnings etc.

• **Differentiation:** Many products are instantly recognisable because of the shape or design of the packaging, some of which are patented and legally protected e.g. Coca-Cola bottle.

Evaluation

Product security can be provided through packaging. Packaging can make items tamper resistant, can help reduce theft and can help prevent harm from dangerous products.

Illustrate what is meant by the product lifecycle and describe the stages of the cycle. (*30 marks*)

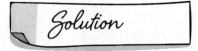

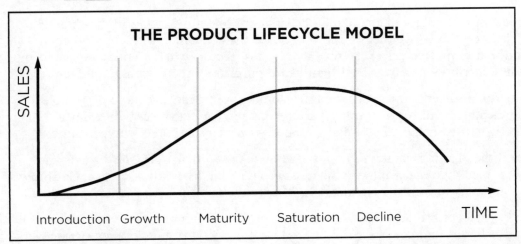

THE PRODUCT LIFECYCLE MODEL

* **Introduction**
  Sales are slow as the product is not yet known. Costs are high due to heavy marketing spend to create awareness. Emphasis is on advertising and distribution. The recently launched **Keogh's Popcorn** is an example.

EXAM WATCH

The chart must be labelled fully and a good description is needed at each stage.

* **Growth**
  This stage shows growing market acceptance and increasing profits. Competitors begin to enter the marketplace. The business concentrates on optimising product availability. **Kerrygold Garlic Bread** range is an example of brand at growth stage.

* **Maturity**
  The rate of sales growth slows down as the product has been widely distributed and sold. The company now focuses on creating brand extensions and promotional offers to boost sales. New product research is critical to ensure future sales. **Cadbury's Snack** range is an example of a brand at the maturity stage.

* **Saturation**
  Sales slow down as the market becomes saturated. Profits level off and may even decline due to increased investment in marketing to defend against competitors. **McDonald's** is an example of a brand that has reached saturation stage.

* **Decline**
  Sales slow down dramatically, and profits fall off. The product may be dropped to make way for new products and the cycle recommences. **Cadbury's Creme Egg** is an example of a brand that has reached the decline stage.

> **Outline the factors a business should consider when choosing a suitable channel of distribution. Provide examples to illustrate your answer.** (*20 marks*)

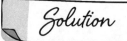

1. **Cost:** Cost is a factor in choice of channel of distribution. The more stages in the channel of distribution, the more expensive the product will be for the consumer, as each middleman will require a cut or mark-up. **Ryanair** was motivated by cost factors when it cut travel agents out of its ticket sales distribution network. **Aldi** and **Lidl** purchase directly from manufacturers.

2. **Type of goods/durability:** Some goods are bulky, others are fragile and more perishable. Perishable goods must be distributed quickly to the market, e.g. **fresh strawberries** are delivered directly to the retailer. High quality products may be sold directly to consumer.

3. **Market size:** If the market is large then using a wholesaler to break bulk, store goods and transport products to the retailer may be the most economical distribution option. **Cadbury's** distributes its products through wholesalers like **Musgrave Group**.

4. **E-business:** Companies can advertise and sell their products online using a company website. Consumers place orders and goods are delivered using the postal system or a courier delivery service. **Asos** is an example.

> **Outline the factors a marketing manager might consider in determining the selling price of branded products in a new Irish clothing range for the teenage market.** (*20 marks*)

The factors include:

*   **Costs:** The price should cover the firm's costs (production, marketing, distribution, etc.) and include a profit margin. Breakeven analysis will help here to find the breakeven point and target profit levels.

*   **Competitors' prices:** Competition is very intense in the clothing industry and this will influence the price to be charged. The pricing plateau for the product is a strong consideration, however, the Irish clothing company could opt for a low pricing strategy in order to capture market share from competitors.

> **EXAM WATCH**
>
> It is wise to refer to the business or product in your answer.

*   **Type of product/image:** As the business is selling branded clothing for the teenage market, the price may be set at a high rate to reflect consumers' perception of a high quality, must-have product.

*   **Stage of product lifecycle:** As the products are new and at the introductory stage, a high price may be charged to help recover R&D costs and to give the impression of a superior brand.

> **Describe four pricing strategies used by firms, giving an example of each strategy.** (*25 marks*)

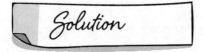

Pricing Strategies

1. Cost-based pricing – this can either simply cover costs or include an element of profit. It focuses on the product and does not take account of consumers.
   - **Restaurants** tend to add on 70% to cost of food raw materials to find the price.

2. Penetration price – an initial low price to ensure that there is a high volume of purchases and market share is quickly won. This strategy encourages consumers to develop a habit of buying.
   - **Own brand craft beers** are an example of this strategy.

3. Price skimming – an initial high price for a unique product, encouraging those who want to be 'first to buy' to pay a premium price. This strategy helps a business to gain maximum revenue before a competitor's product reaches the market.
   - The **Apple iWatch** is an example.

4. Psychological pricing – psychological pricing is a pricing/marketing strategy based on the theory that certain prices have a psychological impact. Retail prices are often expressed as 'odd prices': a little less than a round number, e.g. €19.99 or €2.98.
   - **Penneys** uses this strategy.

> **Explain the term 'market segmentation' and explain three methods used to divide a market.** (*20 marks*)

Market segmentation involves dividing up the market into clearly identifiable **sections**, which have common characteristics. It allows a firm to identify who their target market is, e.g. the targeted section for **Fredo bars** is younger children without income.

- Demographic segmentation separates your audience by **who they are,** using the following traits: age gender occupation income family status
  Example: **Expensive jewellery** is targeted at families with high disposable incomes.

- Geographical segmentation is best used when a customer's **location** influences their purchase **decision**. This is going to be true for nearly any business, which is why geographical segmentation is one of the most popular forms of segmentation used.
  Example: **Marks & Spencer's** pre-prepared luxury foods are aimed at urban dwellers more than rural shoppers.

– continued overleaf

- <u>Psychographic segmentation</u> separates the market audience by their **personality.** For example, interests, attitudes, values and lifestyle. This can be especially useful for businesses which sell a product or service that will make an impact on people with specific world views or ideas.

  Example: People who would typically buy **Green & Black's** ethically sourced chocolate.

Define public relations and outline three methods used by Irish businesses. (*20 marks*)

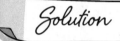

Public relations describes the various methods a company uses to disseminate messages about its products, services, or **overall image** to its customers, employees, investors, suppliers, or other interested members of the community. A more favourable image ultimately leads to **higher sales and profits.** The point of public relations is to make the public **think favourably** about the company and its offerings.

The use of current examples impresses the corrector.

Methods used include:

- <u>Sponsorship</u>

  Sponsorship is a form of public relations where businesses pay money so that their product name will be displayed by individuals, organisations or at particular events, e.g. **Dubai Duty Free** sponsors the **Irish Derby horse racing festival** at The Curragh. This is in line with the firm's global strategy of promoting both their own duty-free brand and the city of Dubai itself. This sponsorship enables the firm **to reach its potential audience** and to speak to them through the medium of exciting, premium sport.

- <u>Celebrity endorsement</u>

  Endorsements are a form of public relations that use famous personalities or celebrities who command a high degree of recognition, trust, respect, or awareness amongst people. Such celebrities advertise a product, lending their names or images to promote a product or service. Oscar winner **Kate Winslet** has had a long-term endorsement deal as '**Ambassador of Elegance**' for luxury watchmaker **Longines.**

- <u>Charitable work and donations</u>

  Public relations departments of firms organise fundraising events to highlight the existence of a chosen charity and make significant financial contributions. For example, **Domino's** delivering 200,000 slices of pizza for **Feed the Heroes** and people in need during the COVID-19 pandemic.

UNIT

6

Notes

Unit 6

> John and Mary want to set up their own beauty salon on the main street of their own hometown. They heard that forming a company would be a good idea.
>
> Advise the couple on the opportunities and risks attached to the idea. *(20 marks)*

Advantages

- Limited Liability

  This concept is of particular benefit to smaller investors in the event of things going wrong, e.g. they may only lose a maximum of what they had invested and not their private wealth.

- Corporate Status

  The company would have separate legal status from John and Mary, and can sue and be sued in its own name. Once they obey the Companies Act, they are not held personally liable for the debts of the business.

Disadvantages

- Legal Costs

  It costs about €800 in legal fees to set up a private limited company and this can prove to be expensive for a small business. There are also accounting charges.

- Taxation

  If the company makes a profit, it is liable for corporation tax. If John and Mary are employees, which they will be, they will be liable for Pay As You Earn (PAYE). If they receive dividends, they will also be taxed.

> Outline four advantages of indigenous Irish firms. *(20 marks)*

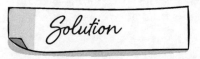

Indigenous firms are set up in Ireland by Irish people. They are home-based and home-owned; they are not multinational companies. They are promoted by the State-sponsored body, Enterprise Ireland. E.g. **Supermac's**.

The advantages are:

- These firms are loyal to the Irish economy

  Unlike multinational companies, these firms tend to stay in Ireland during harsh economic times. They do not look for cheaper labour abroad, and have a social responsibility to the Irish people. These firms have a direct interest in the wellbeing of the Irish economy.

– continued overleaf

- These firms promote an enterprise culture

  Indigenous firms foster the spirit of enterprise in Ireland. They encourage people to take the initiative and this reduces our dependence on foreign companies. Small Irish businesses are given every opportunity to supply larger, Irish-owned firms.

- These firms create employment

  Irish firms create direct jobs at home and contribute greatly to wealth production in the Irish economy, e.g. **Supermac's employs 2,700 people in the Republic of Ireland**. These wages are spent in the economy, creating a knock-on or multiplier effect, which indirectly creates jobs.

- Profits are kept at home

  Unlike multinational companies, which tend to repatriate their profits (i.e. send them home), the wealth generated by indigenous firms tends to stay in the Irish economy. The activities of indigenous firms boost economic growth in Ireland.

EXAM WATCH

Musgrave and **Green Isle Foods** are useful examples of successful Irish indigenous firms.

Contrast a Private Limited Company (company limited by shares) with a Public Limited Company as a form of business organisation. (*20 marks*)

Solution

- Number of members

  A private limited company has a minimum of one shareholder and a maximum of 149. A public limited company has a minimum of seven shareholders and no maximum.

- Transfer of shares

  A private limited company has a restriction on the transfer of shares. A public limited company has its shares bought and sold freely on the stock exchange.

- Publishing of information

  Small and medium-sized private companies only needed to publish restricted versions of their final accounts. All public limited companies must publish a full set of final accounts.

- Cost of formation

  A private company can be set up for as little as €800 but to become a public company, certain Stock Exchange regulations must be met, and a financial institution has to back the share issue, i.e. buy surplus shares. There are also expensive public relations fees.

List four programmes that promote community development. (*10 marks*)

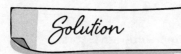

- Area Partnership Company
- Local Enterprise Office
- LEADER +
- SOLAS

EXAM WATCH

Only use these specific agencies.

Describe how the services provided by one community development organisation in your locality helps business enterprises. (*20 marks*)

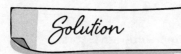

The **Local Enterprise Office (LEO)** is the '*First Stop Shop*' for anyone seeking information and support on starting or growing a business in Ireland. The Local Enterprise Office provides advice, information, and support to entrepreneurs in starting-up or growing a business.

- **Support and advice**

  The LEO provides a full information and advice service to expanding and potential entrepreneurs on all aspects of setting up and running a business. LEOs are a first port of call for those needing information and advice on how to go about setting up or expanding a micro business venture.

- **'Soft' supports**

  Critically important success factors, for enhancing business growth include knowledge and intellectual input, and skills/expertise. The range of 'soft' supports on offer can vary from LEO to LEO but would typically include training programmes, workshops, seminars, and mentoring services, e.g. Limerick LEO offers heavily subsidised training courses to help aspiring entrepreneurs.

- **Mentoring**

  A significant and much utilised component of the 'soft' support intervention of LEOs is their mentor programme. This particular programme seeks to match up the knowledge, skills, insights and entrepreneurial capability of experienced business practitioners with small business owners who need practical help.

- **Feasibility grants**

  These may be provided to assist with the cost of necessary pre-start-up studies carried out for the purposes of assessing market interest in, and demand for, a proposed new product or service; the appropriateness of the associated funding plans; and the general viability and sustainability of the venture. The maximum feasibility grant available is €15,000.

> Analyse how the economic variables (factors) in the Irish economy have an impact on a local economy. (*20 marks*)

The performance of the Irish economy has a huge bearing on Irish business. We will look at the key economic variables and their effect on a local economy.

EXAM WATCH

Definition of each economic variable needed, plus their impact on the local economy.

1. **Interest Rates (currently -0.5%)**

   This is the cost of borrowing. It depends on the demand and supply of money and is measured as a percentage.

   A *low interest rate* means that it is cheap for firms to borrow money.

   • They will expand, creating jobs
   • Consumers will borrow and spend
   • Firms are more profitable

   This boosts the local economy as the cost of credit is lower for consumers and investors.

2. **Inflation (currently 0.7%)**

   This is a sustained growth in the general level of prices based on the Consumer Price Index and the average family.

   Low inflation means:

   • More competitive exports
   • Good for investment in the local economy
   • Better standard of living in the local economy
   • Less Industrial Relations unrest and labour days lost
   • Spending power is boosted in the local economy

3. **Unemployment**

   The rate is 5.4%* (full employment in Ireland is 4.2%)

   This figure has been temporarily distorted due to the coronavirus pandemic and is estimated at 16% if all COVID-19 payment recipients are included.

   • It is the number of people who are available and seek work unsuccessfully
   • Low unemployment is good for business as consumers have greater incomes and therefore **greater purchasing power**. It means **more revenue for government** and **less spending on social welfare.** This boosts the local economy

4. **Taxation**

   • It erodes a consumer's purchasing power (income)
   • It reduces company profits (corporation tax)
   • PRSI increases the cost of employing someone and this reduces job creation potential in the local economy
   • VAT is an extra burden and inconvenience on a business
   • Low tax rates benefit a business and boost the local economy as factory owners and employees are better off financially and have greater disposable incomes

Illustrate environmental and ethical initiatives used by forward-thinking businesses. *(15 marks)*

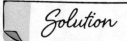

Treatment of stakeholders

The sportswear company Adidas tries to give long-term contracts to its suppliers to improve working relationships. They also put pressure on suppliers to pay adequate wages and overtime pay to their employees.

Environmental issues

Puma has banned the use of hazardous substances in its production processes. The Body Shop 'dedicates itself' to the pursuit of social and environmental change.

EXAM WATCH

It is not sufficient to use 'reduce, reuse, recycle'. Specific examples are more impressive.

Sponsorship

Many firms contribute generously to charities. AIB has a 'Better Ireland' programme which provides educational opportunities for disadvantaged students.

Outline the characteristics of an environmentally conscious business enterprise. *(20 marks)*

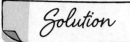

An environmentally conscious firm should be:

Committed: To rectifying all mistakes in the most efficient environmentally friendly way possible, e.g. DCC has implemented production changes to minimise waste.

Honest: It must disclose all relevant facts which may affect the environment, e.g. accidents reported immediately.

Awareness: Promotes environmental issues among its employees, customers and business community, and spends money on the issues.

EXAM WATCH

It is helpful to use the acronym **CHAOS** here, to bring structure to the answer.

Open: To new environmentally-friendly methods and to new ideas, e.g. Greyhound Recycling, a waste management firm, welcomes new ideas from stakeholders.

Sensitive: To all environmental needs, and makes a voluntary effort to incorporate environmental issues into its overall policy, e.g. Nokia makes smaller products and consequently uses less raw materials.

> **Illustrate how firms can be socially responsible.** *(20 marks)*

Solution

Business has social responsibilities to the following:

- **Investors**
  - To act in accordance with its Memorandum and Articles of Association
  - Provide a fair return on the investment by shareholders
  - Avoid excessive payments to senior management
  - To present a true and fair view of the financial performance and standing of the business and maintain a proper set of accounts

  Example: **High risk lending at Anglo Irish Bank was not socially responsible to investors.**

- **Employees**
  - Adhere to Employment Law, Health and Safety regulations, etc
  - Pay a fair wage to all employees
  - Provide a safe working environment
  - Treat employees with dignity and respect/no discrimination
  - Provide equal opportunities for promotion, pay, etc. to all employees

  Example: **Bank of Ireland measures job satisfaction and connectivity to the job. It also believes in providing state-of-the art equipment for employees.**

- **Customers**
  - Fair and honest advertising of its product
  - Abide by health and safety regulations; products must be safe
  - Goods must be of merchantable quality, match their description, be fit for purpose, etc
  - Uphold the right of the customer to complain and to investigate such complaints
  - Good after-sales service
  - Charge a fair price

  Example: **Staff misleading customers by taking deposits for new orders for new furniture even though the business was on the point of liquidation.**

- **Suppliers**
  - Always pay them on time
  - Always give adequate notice when placing an order
  - Use a fair tendering system going for the best quality based on the price charged

  Example: **During the coronavirus crisis, British pub chain JD Wetherspoon suspended payments to its suppliers in the Republic of Ireland until its pubs reopen**

Describe the three categories of industry and describe the current trends in each category. *(25 marks)*

1. The **Primary Sector** (extractive) is a category of industry based on the natural resources of a country, such as agriculture, forestry, fishing, mining, energy.

   Current trends:
   - Commodities such as beef and milk are commanding higher prices on world markets as demand increases due to global population growth.
   - Cóillte, the State agency operating in forestry, land-based businesses, renewable energy and panel products, may be privatised along with other businesses such as Electric Ireland.
   - Producers of beef protesting at the big supermarkets over low profit margins.

2. The **Secondary Sector** includes manufacturing, agribusiness and construction businesses that manufacture products from the materials produced by the primary sector (agriculture, forestry, fishing and mining). It takes raw materials, processes raw materials, and produces finished goods, e.g. Kerry Group – food products.

   Current trends:
   - Decline in employment in secondary sector – downsizing and closures have resulted in an increase in unemployment, particularly in relation to manufacturing.
   - Increased competition – challenge faced by agribusiness sector in the food market from foreign retailers, i.e. Lidl and Aldi

3. The **Tertiary Sector** provides essential backup for primary and secondary sectors. This category is not in the business of 'making' more, by way of consultancy and support services. It includes banking, legal, accounting, insurance and software assistance to name just a few. It includes TV journalism and telecommunications.

   Current trends:
   - The growth of the ICT sector has led to employment opportunities.
   - The growth of e-business (a method of buying and selling goods and services over the internet) is changing the dynamic of the services sector. Retailers moving to on-line operations include Tesco and Next.
   - Brexit uncertainty due to delayed talks between EU and UK has affected consumer confidence and thus lowered the demand for services.

> **Explain how the government through its policies affects the labour force.**
> *(25 marks)*

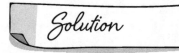

- Improve the Infrastructure

  If the government puts appropriate back-up services in place, it will facilitate business activity and job creation.
  - *€3bn spend on broadband will attract investment to rural Ireland and allow employees to work remotely*

- Lower Taxes

  Low personal taxation (20%) encourages people to get a job, and low corporation tax (12.5%) means that the entrepreneur can afford to hire more labour.
  - *The universal social charge rates have been lowered in recent budgets*
  - *Only Hungary has a lower corporate tax rate than Ireland.*

- Economic Variables, e.g. interest rates

  If the government/ECB keeps interest rates low, the entrepreneur can afford to build more factories. Consumers can afford to buy more goods. This means that more jobs are created.
  - *The marginal lending rate is now -0.5% in the euro area, compared with 4.75% in 2000*

- Future Plans

  The government puts together national plans, which make job creation a priority. The focus is on sustainable jobs in energy, medical devices and tourism, for example.
  - *The action plan for jobs and employment strategy was launched at a time when unemployment was 15%, in 2012*

- Direct Employment

  The government pays the wages of approximately 323,000 employees, who help to successfully run the country. This has a direct impact on the labour force.
  - *This is 15% of the Irish entire workforce*

- Improve Investment and Training

  The government pumps money into specific agencies such as SOLAS and Fáilte Ireland, whose services make people more marketable by improving skills.
  - *€415m was spent under the National Training Fund in 2018*

Outline how ethical behaviour in business can be encouraged. *(15 marks)*

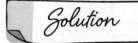

* **Establishing a code of ethics**: A code of ethics is a formal written statement, setting out the modes of behaviour expected from a business in its dealings with employees, customers and the community in which it operates/encourages a culture of openness.

* **Encouraging 'whistleblowing'**: This involves encouraging staff to report unethical behaviour by creating a climate where whistleblowing is rewarded and legislation is put in place to protect the whistleblower.

EXAM WATCH

This answer needs to be pre-prepared and very specific.

* **Modelling ethical behaviour**: When senior staff are highly ethical and model ethical behaviour, it will encourage subordinates to behave in a similar manner.

* **Staff training**: A code of ethics should be presented to staff at induction training and reminder training should include modules on ethical behaviour.

Outline the reasons why a business might change its organisational structure from a sole trader to a private limited company. *(20 marks)*

Changing Circumstances: A sole trader might change their ownership structure to a private limited company over time to adapt to changing circumstances and market demands. Choosing a private limited company as an ownership structure can facilitate the plans that the owner may have for the organisation far into the future and the vision of where the organisation wants to be.

Economies of Scale: The business enterprise might wish to grow. With size comes the burden of extra specialisation, where one individual cannot do all things and more people and expertise are needed, e.g. specialists in finance, marketing, production.

Limited Liability: The desire for the protection of limited liability is another reason for changing structure. A businessperson wishes to protect family members from business risks and ensure a secure future for them. Personal assets must be protected to do this. Reduced risk of personal loss. Private limited companies can now be set up with only one shareholder.

Capital: If more capital is needed for the development of the business, then a move from being a sole trader to a private limited company might be necessary. It is possible to raise the necessary capital through the issue of shares to other shareholders, up to the amount of authorised capital stated in the memorandum of association.

Outline the advantages and disadvantages for a business in the fast food sector of choosing franchising as a method of business expansion. *(20 marks)*

Advantages

- It is a form of expansion which requires low capital investment by the franchisor, as the capital used to expand the business comes from franchisees. Very suitable/popular in the current economic climate as a form of expansion.

- Franchising permits a more rapid expansion. By using the franchisees' capital, the franchisor is able to establish a large number of outlets in a short period of time. Rapid expansion can be achieved without incurring the overheads and costs associated with opening company-owned restaurants.

EXAM WATCH

Know the difference between the franchisor and the franchisee. If a business is named in the question, **always reference the name in the answer**.

- An owner will be more attentive than a manager. This is the central point which makes franchising so attractive. The franchisor can be assured that the person operating its restaurant will be 'attending to business' as much as they would.

- Economies of scale exist. There is strength in numbers. The successful franchisor can command deals with various suppliers and can control supplies to various franchisees. The cost savings can increase the franchisor's profits.

Disadvantages

- Control is lost over the day-to-day management of the franchise businesses. The reputation of the whole business could be affected by the actions of one franchisee/poor quality standards/ staff.

- A training programme for franchisees will be required. This will be expensive and time consuming.

> **Define privatisation and outline the advantages of privatisation.** *(20 marks)*

Privatisation is the selling-off of State-owned enterprises to the private sector.

The arguments in favour of privatisation of commercial state enterprises:

EXAM WATCH

The Irish government sold Bord Gáis in 2014, for €950m, to Centrica a British-based energy company.

* <u>Government Revenue</u>: Selling-off a State enterprise provides the government with a large sum of money, e.g. Aer Lingus.

* <u>Reduced Expenditure</u>: The sale of a loss-making enterprise means it must no longer be subsidised on a yearly basis by the government/less borrowing required by government/money available for other services.

* <u>Efficiency</u>: State-owned enterprises are often perceived as being inefficient because they can rely on government funding and have little competition. Private firms are driven by a profit motive and should, therefore, be more efficiently run.

* <u>Access to Finance</u>: Privatised firms are able to take out loans and shares, and generally have greater access to sources of finance than State enterprise. This makes it easier to fund expansion.

UNIT

7

Notes

Unit 7

> **Explain the decision-making process of the European Union. Include the relevant institutions in your answer.** *(25 marks)*

The EU decision-making process:

- The **EU Commission** proposes a new law. This body oversees the running of the European Union on a daily basis. It consists of EU commissioners appointed by the member states.

- The new law is then discussed by the **European Parliament**, which is sometimes referred to as a 'talking shop'. This institution debates the pros and cons of the proposed new legislation and takes on board the views of special interest groups, e.g. IFA.

- The proposed new law is then passed back to the **EU Commission** and then take on board any useful amendments as decided by the **EU Parliament**. The EU Commission then redrafts the proposed bill.

- The proposed legislation is passed on to the main decision-making body of the EU, which is the **EU Council of Ministers**. This collective institution consists of the various ministers from each member state who are most affected by the new legislation, e.g. the EU Council of Ministers for finance ultimately ratified the euro. The new legislation is accepted or rejected by the European Council of Ministers.

This new legislation, if accepted, **may be implemented by the EU Commission as follows**:

1. Regulations are legal acts that apply automatically and uniformly to all EU countries as soon as they enter into force, without needing to be transposed into national law. They are binding in their entirety on all EU countries, e.g. General Data Protection Regulation (GDPR).

2. Directives require EU countries to achieve a certain result but leave them free to choose how to do so. EU countries must adopt measures to incorporate them into national law (transpose) in order to achieve the objectives set by the directive. National authorities must communicate these measures to the European Commission, e.g. EU Consumer Rights Directive.

3. By decision: This only applies to individual members or companies, e.g. the members of a vitamin cartel were fined €855m for price-fixing.

> **Illustrate the role of special interest groups in the decision-making process of the European Union.** *(15 marks)*

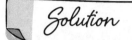

- Irish laws are now made centrally in Europe for us and so, items like a minimum wage, maximum working week, consumer protection and waste reduction, all have a major impact on Irish people. At EU level, we are given a voice by special interest groups.

- These pressure groups are representative organisations and are outside of the Irish and European political systems, but exert pressure on the lawmakers by lobbying them on a range of issues which affect ordinary people.

- These interest groups conduct campaigns in the press, on television and on radio to ensure that the voices which they represent are heard by the decision-makers, e.g. **Irish Farmers Association (IFA)** lobbying against unfavourable farming law changes. These interest groups lobby MEPs, commissioners and EU civil servants.

- **2,600 special interest groups have offices in Brussels.**

> **Distinguish between each of the following EU institutions:**
> - **European Commission**
> - **EU Council of Ministers**
> - **European Parliament**
> - **European Court of Auditors**
>
> *(40 marks)*

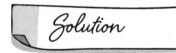

European Commission
- This body consists of commissioners who are appointed by the member states.
- This body oversees the **implementation of new legislation.**
- It manages the daily affairs of the EU.
- It defends EU interests at world level.

EU Council of Ministers
- This is the **main decision-making body of the European Union.**
- It decides which policies to adopt and which laws to implement.
- It co-ordinates national policies of the member states.
- It controls the EU budget.
- All legislation must be passed by the council.

European Parliament

- This democratically elected body is often referred to as being a 'talking shop'.
- This is due to its propensity towards discussion rather than its ability to act.
- It monitors the performance of the EU Commission.
- It gives advice to the EU Commission.

European Court of Auditors

- This institution monitors the usage of the EU budget.
- It carries out random spot checks on various projects throughout the EU.
- It prepares financial reports.
- It tries to eliminate the wasting of funds and to reduce levels of fraud.

> **Outline the opportunities and challenges for Irish business as a result of engaging in foreign trade.** *(30 marks)*

Opportunities for Irish business in foreign/international trade:

- Access to Bigger Markets: Export markets provide a larger potential market for a firm and provide an opportunity to increase sales and profits. The EU post-Brexit has a population of 446m.
- Economies of Scale: An economy of scale reduces cost per unit as a firm increases in size, i.e. reductions in costs that come from buying, producing and selling in large quantities.
- Reduced Risk: By diversifying into a new market, a firm is spreading its risk, making it less dependent on one market.
- Free Movement of Services, Labour and Capital: The Irish construction sector benefited hugely from the availability of Polish and other EU workers during the boom years. Business may also source the best investment opportunities in the EU.
- Workforce: We have a well-educated young workforce with up-to-date skills, which gives us a competitive advantage in high-tech areas and a well-developed knowledge economy.

Challenges for Irish business in foreign/international trade:

- Competition: Traditionally, the Irish government would have protected the 'infant' industry from the full force of competition through trade barriers. Deregulation of EU markets means that only competitive firms will survive, and this may affect employment here.
- Development of Human Resources: Training and development programmes will have to be introduced as, apart from the highly competitive markets (in which strikes would have serious implications), we also have language problems, marketing changes and the introduction of technology to deal with.
- Costs: Our geographical location at the edge of Europe means that we have extra transport and greater distribution costs. We should hope that a focus on quality, and improvements in technology and logistics would help us overcome this challenge.

> **Describe how the changing nature of the international economy affects Irish business.** *(30 marks)*

The main changes that affect Irish businesses are:

• World Trade Organisation

This was set up post-World War II as the General Agreement on Tariffs and Trade, and has been hugely successful at opening up markets to free trade. This is very important for an export-orientated country like Ireland.

  • **96% of our GDP comes from exports**

• The European Union

We are part of an economic trading bloc, which has grown in strength since Economic and Monetary Union (EMU). This offers benefits and opportunities for Ireland and operates a trading area without barriers that has common external tariffs on outsiders.

  • **It is the third largest market in the world**

• Transnationals (TNCs)

We live in a world of global business and a single brand worldwide. The attraction of these companies to Ireland has been high on IDA Ireland's priority list and gives massive employment.

  • **It is estimated that €8bn is the annual payroll from TNCs and they spend €23bn in the economy.**

• Technology

This has rendered location to be less important and developments should reduce transport costs. The use of 'logistics' is becoming more common. Much of our exports are technology-related, as we have concentrated on the knowledge economy.

  • **8 of the top 10 firms in ICT,**
  • **8 of the top 10 firms in Pharmaceuticals,**
  • **15 of the top 25 firms in Medical Devices have all set up in Ireland**

• Emerging countries

The development of the Pacific Rim and South American countries, e.g. China and Brazil, that are producing high quality, low-cost goods, will prove a threat to EU countries. Ireland must concentrate on high-tech industries.

• Brexit

The possibility of a no deal Brexit would mean that Irish exporters to the UK would face protectionist measures. 40% of Irish agribusiness exports currently go to the UK.

Discuss the role of trading blocs for trade. Illustrate your answer with an example. *(30 marks)*

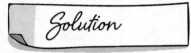

- A trading bloc is a group of countries that organises a free trade area amongst themselves, to promote trade and to eliminate barriers such as tariffs and quotas, e.g. **the European Union**.

- The European Union has free movement of goods, services, labour and capital, which facilitates trade among members and shows preference to EU output, using common external tariffs on non-members.

- The EU has had a huge impact on trade for Ireland, which is a small, open economy, which relies heavily on foreign trade. Our combined exports and imports exceed our national income.

- We have access to a market of 446 million people, which provides great opportunities for exports. We now send 50% of our exports to other countries in the trading bloc.

- Deregulation of markets within the EU has allowed Irish firms that produce high quality goods and services to prosper, as only the best and most efficient will survive. This has meant lower prices and better quality for consumers in the EU, e.g. price of airline tickets has fallen significantly.

Outline the purpose of the European Union's competition policy. *(10 marks)*

- The purpose of the policy is to ensure **uniform practices in businesses** throughout the European Union, and to outlaw agreements which prevent, restrict or distort trade and eliminate fair competition.

- It prevents cartels and unfair trading practices, e.g. in the cement industry and vitamin tablet industry, whereby consumers were being cheated by unscrupulous producers who **fixed prices and carved up markets between them.**

- Competition stimulates **innovation and efficiency** among businesses, and consumers' best interests are safeguarded, e.g. Aer Lingus has reduced its commission to travel agents and thus benefiting the consumer.

> **Explain the benefits of Economic and Monetary Union membership for Irish business.** *(20 marks)*

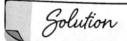

The main advantages of Economic and Monetary Union (EMU) are a reduction in transaction costs and an end to **destabilising currency shifts** within Europe. The elimination of these **transaction costs** benefits a country like Ireland whose businesses export a considerable amount of its output to the European Union. Currency fluctuation problems have been eliminated on trade within the euro area.

EXAM WATCH

This question is not a general question on the European Union and the answer must reference EMU and the euro at all stages. A common mistake is to call EMU European monetary union.

A single currency highlights price differential. Businesses sourcing raw materials and components can readily identify the **best bargains** throughout the EU.

The European Central Bank (ECB) has a monetary policy that focuses on price stability. This includes setting interest rates for the euro zone. Record **low interest rates** set by the ECB of late facilitate business expansion and investment. Sustained periods of low inflation are good for Irish business.

Ireland's common currency is an attraction for foreign direct investment (FDI) because trade within a large European market is less bureaucratic and relatively cheap. Increased FDI has positive spin-off effects for Irish indigenous industry. It is one of the main reasons for FDI companies setting up here.

> **Explain how important the European Union is to Ireland.** *(15 marks)*

Solution

- Enlarged Markets: The European Union has given Irish producers the opportunity to gain access to a market of 446 million and to trade in an area without barriers. These enlarged markets allow smaller Irish companies to benefit from large-scale production and the resulting cost savings, i.e. economies of scale.

- Financial Aid: Over the past 30 years, for every 1% that we contributed to the European Union budget we received 11%. Ireland was a net beneficiary of the EU until 2014. This money was used to upgrade our infrastructure and to make us attractive to foreign investors, e.g. the 1,550 transnational companies would not have been attracted by 1973 Ireland.

- Single Currency and Economic and Monetary Union: We now have closer economic and political ties throughout the EU. Uniform interest rates, free movement of capital and labour, and a single currency have facilitated trade and tourism. As we have a small, open economy this has had a major impact.

> **Define 'protectionism' and outline three barriers to trade in international trade.**
> *(20 marks)*

Protectionism involves governments protecting their own economies by erecting barriers to trade. The following are the main methods used:

- Tariffs

  These are **taxes on imports** which make them more expensive and so help the domestic producer. The EU does not place tariffs on the world's poorest 49 countries, to help them to develop. **E.g. Apples from China to EU: 9%.**

- Quotas

  These are **a limit** on the amount of an import that can enter a country. A quota is **a numerical restriction** and is designed to help indigenous business. The EU quota on processed **chicken imports from Thailand** is 160,000 tonnes per year.

- Embargoes

  These are a **complete ban** on trade with a specific country, e.g. the **European Union's** sanctions against Burma (Myanmar), based on lack of democracy and human rights infringements.

> **Distinguish between 'standardised market' and 'adapted market' as relating to global marketing.** *(20 marks)*

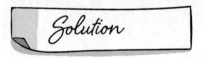

Global marketing treats the world as being **one single marketplace.** The goods can be standardised or adapted, depending on circumstances.

- Standardised:
  - Undifferentiated approach to the 4 Ps/consistent marketing mix.
  - Global businesses, like **Nike and Marlboro,** with successful brands, aim to take the same, undifferentiated approach worldwide, and use a standardised marketing mix. All products are targeted at similar groups locally. This leads to **lower company costs and increased profitability**.

- Adapted marketing mix:
  - Some element(s) of the marketing mix (product, price promotion and place) is/are changed to reflect local customs, values, and economic situations.
  - It is common for business to adapt the marketing mix to reflect regional differences, local language, cultural, geographic, or economic differences present in the market, e.g. **McDonald's Chicken Maharaja Mac in India.**

'NIGHT BEFORE' NOTES OR POINTERS

Short Answer Questions
20% of the Higher Level Paper

Advice

- **Over answer the definitions questions**
- **Always label diagrams**
- **Write true or false in FULL**
- **Use examples when required**
- **Answer all 10 questions**

METHOD FOR
ABQs

1. Read the questions before reading the passage

2. Jot down the main headings at the back of your answer book

3. Read the passage at least twice

4. The links are usually very obvious

5. Name, explain and link

6. You can use the same link in separate questions A and B and C, if relevant

7. If 'discuss' is the outcome verb, write mini paragraphs

Chapter 1	☐ Make sure of the TWO relationships ☐ Remember to use **MUTUAL BENEFIT** for co-operative relationship ☐ Know the basics on **each stakeholder** ☐ Watch for separate question on **INTEREST GROUPS**
Chapter 2	☐ Know Contract elements, termination and remedies for breach ☐ Invitation to Treat last asked 2008 ☐ Legislative v Non-Legislative methods of conflict resolution ☐ Consumer Acts and functions of CCPC ☐ Merchantable Quality needs reference to **Price and Durability** ☐ Guarantee is an **Additional benefit**
Chapter 3	☐ Employment Discrimination: include **LESS FAVOURABLE** in the answer ☐ Methods of Industrial action ☐ Know Primary and Secondary Picketing ☐ Know Negotiation, Arbitration and Conciliation ☐ Labour legislation and WRC
Chapter 4	☐ Watch for **Intrapreneurship** ☐ Do not confuse **Managerial words** with entrepreneurial words ☐ <u>Keep list simple for enterprise characteristics/skills</u> ☐ Innovative ☐ Risk Taker ☐ Independent ☐ Realistic ☐ Confident ☐ Flexible
Chapter 5	☐ Know Leadership definition ☐ Styles: Autocratic, Democratic and Laissez-Faire ☐ Know Maslow's Hierarchy of Human Needs in exact order ☐ Know McGregor Theory X and Y
Chapter 6	☐ Know Principles of good communications ☐ Know Barriers to effective communications ☐ Reports, Memo and letter ☐ Remember **Data Protection Act** can be examined in UNIT ONE ☐ Mention **Technology types** first if asked to describe

Chapter 7	☐ Planning definition
	☐ Strategic, Tactical and Contingency
	☐ SWOT and Mission Statement
	☐ Organising: key areas
	☐ Span of control
	☐ Chain of command
	☐ Matrix structure
	☐ Line structure
	☐ Know the three main Control types:
	☐ **Stock**
	☐ **Credit**
	☐ **Quality**
Chapter 8	☐ Formula
	☐ Figures
	☐ Answer
	☐ Comment: trend and accurate analysis needed
	☐ 6 ratios
	☐ Know Profitability, Liquidity and Debt-Equity
	☐ **Practise these unaided**
Chapter 9	☐ Know exact definitions of Tax types
	☐ Watch for Tax calculation as a **SAQ**
	☐ Know tax credit and tax rate
Chapter 10	☐ Know Matching rule
	☐ 3 Sources of Finance types
	☐ Cash flow forecasts
	☐ Bank Loan applications
Chapter 11	☐ Know Risk management and Strategies to **REDUCE** risk
	☐ Know FIVE principles of Insurance
	☐ Average Clause is not a principle (Part of Indemnity)
	☐ Know Business Types
	☐ Know full definition of **Proposal Form**
Chapter 12	☐ Know the functions of HRM, especially **Staff Development**
	☐ **Know the various definitions**
	☐ Be able to link Employee Participation to the following:
	1. Intrapreneurship 2. Empowerment
	3. Democratic leadership 4. Facilitator
	5. Delegation 6. Theory Y

Chapter 13	☐ Know Empowerment: risks and opportunities
	☐ Total Quality Management
	☐ Strategies used to implement change
	☐ Employee involvement
	☐ Job rotation
	☐ Job enrichment
	☐ Job Enlargement
Chapter 14	☐ Sources of Ideas
	☐ Market Research
	☐ Purpose of market research maybe for a healthy product
	☐ Stages of New Product Development
	☐ Breakeven analysis
	☐ How to do table and chart
	☐ Margin of safety **definition**
	☐ **Breakeven Formula**
Chapter 15	☐ Niche market = Specialist
	☐ Segment = Section
	☐ Strategy = Plan
	☐ Marketing v Selling
Chapter 16	☐ **Product** includes Extras, design, brand, lifecycle and packaging
	☐ **Price** includes Strategies and Factors when setting a price
	☐ **Place** means Channels of Distribution (Factors)
Chapter 17	☐ Promotional mix
	☐ **Know the definitions of:**
	☐ Advertising
	☐ Personal Selling
	☐ Sales promotion
	☐ Public Relations and Sponsorship
Chapter 18	☐ Know factors when choosing a source of finance
	☐ Good examples of Types of Production
	☐ Business plan benefits and layout
Chapter 19	☐ **Know this chapter very well**
	☐ Debt v equity as a means of funding an **expansion**
	☐ Exact definitions of mergers and takeovers
	☐ Franchisor v franchisee

Chapter 20	☐ Know the THREE Categories of industry ☐ Know Current trends on each
Chapter 21	☐ Community development ☐ Know **Social** and **Economic** benefits ☐ Know the FOUR agencies
Chapter 22	☐ Business and Society ☐ Social responsibility to stakeholders, ☐ Only use specifically prepared material in exam ☐ 4 Rs are only one point
Chapter 23	☐ Know the IMPACT of Business on the Economy ☐ Know the IMPACT of Economic Variables on BUSINESS ☐ Know how the Government regulates the economy for business
Chapter 24	☐ Know the **10 TYPES** of Business Organisations ☐ Know the various **agencies** involved ☐ Watch for **Franchising** as a Question
Chapter 25	☐ Be very specific on the INSTITUTIONS ☐ Know the exact POLICIES ☐ **Know the EU decision-making process in full**
Chapter 26	☐ Know Visible and Invisible trade ☐ Know Balance of trade and balance of payments ☐ Methods of protectionism, especially a **subsidy**
Chapter 27	☐ Global market a single market of STANDARDISED goods ☐ Know Standardised v Adapted goods ☐ Know the specific **global angle** to the Marketing Mix

APPLIED BUSINESS QUESTIONS
(Suitable for 2022 LCHL)

The areas included here are:
→ **(A) Sources of new business ideas**
→ **(B) Business taxation**
→ **(C) Types of organisations**

- A POINT plus EXPLANATION, plus a LINK from the passage of RELEVANT KNOWLEDGE

- 4 points needed for Part A; will gain full marks

- 4 points were needed for Part B;
  NAME / INFORMATION / LINK

- 4 points needed at Part C;
  2 benefits and 2 drawbacks,
  POINT + EXPLANATION + LINK

- **Relevant knowledge is needed but if enough individual correct points are not given then it is impossible to gain full marks. If you are in any doubt include the extra expanded point.**

Vineport Inn Ltd.

Helen always had a love of travel and it was on one of these trips in 2005 that her most successful idea to date was spawned. She noticed that a series of 'theme' hotels had been established in the South of England. Each hotel catered for the needs and wants of the lover of fine wines and foods.

In previous business ventures she would have relied on meetings of her staff to stimulate the creative process. Helen also relied heavily on consumer feedback to generate new ideas.

The business 'Vineport Inn Ltd' has built up a steady customer base of tourists and repeats. The full-time workforce has grown to 55 and the business reported a net margin of 14% on sales of €2m.

Helen has campaigned against the excise duties on wine, which she maintains is affecting margins at a time when the smoking ban is taking its toll. She also feels that the arrival of the Euro has made prices more transparent across Europe and feels that the Irish government should reduce the Value Added Tax on restaurants. Still with a highly efficient business and above average margins, she knows that other businesses in the industry are worse off than hers.

Helen had operated as a sole trader for the first 18 months but changed to private limited company status in November 2006. She wished to protect her own private wealth and knows that she has the option of bringing in new shareholders in the future. On the downside though, the transition was relatively expensive, and she feels that the business is victim to an unfair tax system.

(A) Outline four sources of new business ideas/opportunities that Helen uses to develop her businesses. Refer to the above text in your answer. *(30 marks)*

Solution

The main sources are:

- Foreign Travel

  Helen has spotted an unusual idea while on holidays and modified the idea to suit the Irish market. She has used her love for travel to explore new ideas. "*She noticed that a series of 'theme' hotels had been established in the South of England.*"

- Brainstorming

  This is a technique whereby a group of staff usually go to an offsite location and discuss a variety of new ideas for a fixed time period and must come up with something tangible. "*In previous business ventures she would have relied on meetings of her staff to stimulate the creative process.*"

- Customer Feedback

  As all business strives to satisfy the consumers' needs and wants profitably it makes good business sense to take their opinions on board. "*Helen also relied heavily on consumer feedback to generate new ideas.*"

- Hobbies and Interests

  Helen has turned a passion and a leisure activity into a profitable business idea. She has carried out the research inadvertently and is now well placed to be successful. "*Helen always had a love of travel and it was on one of these trips in 2005 that her most successful idea to date was spawned.*"

> **(B) Outline the various taxes that Vineport Inn Ltd. should be familiar with. Refer to the above text in your answer.** *(30 marks)*

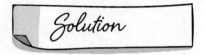

Vineport Inn Ltd. would be familiar with the following type of taxes:

- Corporation Tax
  - This is a tax on a company's profits.
  - It is based on Sales – Allowable Expenses, e.g. wages.
  - The EU standard rate is 12.5%. 'Ltd' means Vineport is a registered company.
  - *"Helen had operated as a sole trader for the first 18 months but changed to private limited company status in November 2006."*

- Value Added Tax (VAT)
  - The business is primarily a retail outlet. It collects this tax on sales and pays it out on purchases. The difference is sent to the Revenue Commissioners.
  - The top rate in Ireland is 21%.⋆
  - *"She also feels that the arrival of the Euro has made prices more transparent across Europe and feels that the Irish government should reduce the Value Added Tax on restaurants."*

- Pay As You Earn (PAYE)
  - Vineport has 55 employees and would have to deduct this tax from their incomes. PAYE is charged on Gross Pay and the employee's tax credit reduces the tax liability. In Ireland the rates are 20% and 40%.
  - *"The full-time workforce has grown to 55."*

- **Excise Duties**
  - This type of tax affects the 'old reliables', which includes alcohol, and this is collected on sales from customers but is bad for business as it pushes up prices.
  - *"Helen has campaigned against the excise duties on wine, which she maintains is affecting margins at a time when the smoking ban is taking its toll."*

⋆ Rate correct at time of going to print. As part of the July 2020 stimulus package during the Covid-19 pandemic, the Irish government temporarily reduced the standard rate of VAT from 23% to 21% for a six-month period, from 1 September 2020 to 28 February 2021.

(C) Explain the benefits and drawbacks for Helen of converting to private company status. Refer to the above text in your answer. *(20 marks)*

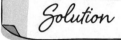

Advantages

• Limited Liability

This concept is of particular benefit to smaller investors in the event of things going wrong, e.g. Helen may only lose a maximum of what she had invested and not her private wealth. "*She wished to protect her own private wealth.*"

• Corporate Status

The company would have separate legal status from Helen and can sue and by sued in its own name. Once they obey the Companies Act, they are not held personally liable for the debts of the business. "*Helen is separate in the eyes of the law than Vineport Inn.*"

Disadvantages

• Legal costs

It costs about €800 in legal fees to set up a private limited company and this can prove to be expensive for a small business. There are also accounting charges. "*On the downside though the transition was relatively expensive.*"

• Taxation

If the company makes a profit it is liable for corporation tax. If Helen is an employee, she will be liable for Pay As You Earn. If she receives dividends, they will also be taxed. "*She feels that the business is victim to an unfair tax system.*"

Wrapido Ltd.

Seamus Foley has recently set up his café and deli counter close to the International Financial Services Centre in Dublin city centre. He had previously worked as head chef for one of the country's leading banks and noticed the phenomenal demand for healthy eating and an overall shift away from the traditional tasty but fatty foods.

He quickly developed his 'Wrapido' brand, which describes both the core ingredient and the notion of speed of service for the overworked financial services worker. The healthy 'wrap' is quickly replacing the 'heavier' rolls and baguettes. The unique selling point focuses on healthy ingredients prepared to order for the discerning customer. This niche market attracts a customer who does not mind paying extra for the added health benefits and the target market is definitely not the mass produced 'breakfast roll' market. Health factors and superior quality are the order of the day. The initial advertising spend has centred on the free morning papers aimed at the thousands of commuters that flock to the area each day. This has been backed up by the regular distribution of flyers in the area.

Six months down the line, Seamus is aware that he has a profitable venture up and running but is struggling to balance his cash inflows and outflows on a daily basis. The acid test ratio is showing at .7:1 whereas net margin is a healthy 25%.

Further analysis has shown that the business is carrying too much stock of raw materials and this is tying up cash. Seamus has no credit control policy in place to collect the outstanding monies from corporate clients that buy in bulk but settling patterns tend to be erratic. The overall liquidity position needs to be overhauled.

Seamus is very aware of the significant impact that the business has on its stakeholders and is anxious to do the right thing by them. He looks for feedback from customers at every opportunity and even welcomes criticisms. Employees are paid 1.5 times the minimum wage, as Seamus sees their satisfaction as the only lasting means of business success. He carefully sources his suppliers and settles his bills promptly, even to the detriment of his own cash position. He is anxious to forge links with the local community and personally takes part in a 'Meals on Wheels' run every Friday morning. His expertise is proving to be invaluable.

(A) Analyse the components of the 'Marketing Mix' of the Wrapido. Refer to the text to support your answer. *(30 marks)*

Solution

Product: The product Wrapido is aimed at the ever-growing number of health-conscious people who like their food to taste great, without piling on the pounds at the same time. It satisfies the needs and wants of the healthy eater. The product lifecycle is at the growth stage and the brand name is well known locally.

"…and noticed the phenomenal demand for healthy eating and an overall shift away from the traditional tasty but fatty foods."

Price: The price was set at a standard €5 per wrap with no limit on fillings. This was in line with market rival O Brien's and also considers the fact that 'green' consumers are prepared to pay more for the health benefits. It takes its own profit margin into account.

"This niche market attracts a customer who does not mind paying extra for the added health benefits and the target market is definitely not the mass produced 'breakfast roll' market."

– continued overleaf

Place: As the product is perishable and targeting a local market, it makes more sense to sell through its retail outlet which is close to the busy offices. The manufacturer-to-customer channel is the most suitable.

"...*the thousands of commuters that flock to the area each day.*"

Promotion: The notion of highlighting the existence of the business with a view to increasing sales is been handled efficiently as it is focusing the spend on a specific target market and is communicating directly with the relevant customers.

"*The initial advertising spend has centred on the free morning papers aimed at the thousands of commuters that flock to the area each day. This has been backed up by the regular distribution of flyers in the area.*"

> **(B) Analyse the firm's liquidity position and offer suggestions based on your findings.** *(25 marks)*

The firm is profitable but there is a cash flow problem **as the acid test ratio is only .7:1**. This means that for every € that falls due in the short term this firm only has 70c to meet it. The ideal situation is that the firm has a ratio of 1:1.

Most firms have cash flow problems due to poor working capital management. It has a poor stock control policy and its cash is being spent on stocks of goods that are not needed in the immediate future. It has a poor credit control policy and is unable to collect the outstanding monies owed to it. Debtors would be 'leaning' on its business and this drains its cash flow.

"*Further analysis has shown that the business is carrying too much stock of raw materials and this is tying up cash. Seamus has no credit control policy in place to collect the outstanding monies from corporate clients that buy in bulk but settling patterns tend to be erratic.*"

Suggestions:

- It could introduce a 'Just in Time' stock policy whereby stocks arrive as closely as possible to the time of use and this releases cash for other areas of the business.

- It could implement a more careful credit policy. It could get credit references on its debtors to minimise slow payments and bad debts. The fact that the business is profitable with a net margin of 25% tells us that the revenues that the firm SHOULD receive and the expenditure that the firm SHOULD pay.

(C) Outline how the business is dealing with social responsibility and its stakeholders. Refer to the text to support your answer. *(25 marks)*

Business has social responsibilities to the following:

- **Investors**

A business has a responsibility to its owners and by creating wealth in the form of profits. It should pay the highest dividend possible. Irish investors can take advantage of ethical investment options. It should retain earnings for the future and manage the return on investment very carefully.

"Six months down the line, Seamus is aware that he has a profitable venture up and running, but is struggling to balance his cash inflows and outflows on a daily basis."

- **Employees**

Workers are not exploited and are paid a fair wage. Conditions are above average, and health and safety issues are a priority. In return, the socially responsible firm benefits from a loyal and productive workforce.

"Employees are paid 1.5 times the minimum wage, as Seamus sees their satisfaction as the only lasting means of business success."

- **Customers**

The business does not exploit and manipulate customers.

Products should not be dangerous and the firm refrains from harmful business practices. In return, they benefit from a loyal and regular custom from socially responsible customers.

"He looks for feedback from customers at every opportunity and even welcomes criticisms."

- **Society**

Business and society should sort out all conflicts and contentious areas and a happy medium of good for business/good for society should be reached. Do we have low unemployment and high pollution or vice versa? The general public are co-operative towards socially responsible firms and give them their business and do not object to expansion

"He is anxious to forge links with the local community and personally takes part in a 'Meals on Wheels' run every Friday morning. His expertise is proving to be invaluable."

Key Revision Tables

Enterprise Words
- ☐ Independent
- ☐ Risk-taker
- ☐ Innovative
- ☐ Opportunistic
- ☐ Future-focused
- ☐ Decisive
- ☐ Proactive
- ☐ Confident

Management Skills
- ☐ Leadership
- ☐ Communicating
- ☐ Motivation

Management Activities
- ☐ Planning
- ☐ Organising
- ☐ Controlling

Types of Planning
- ☐ Strategic
- ☐ Tactical
- ☐ Contingency
- ☐ Mission Statement

Leadership Styles
- ☐ Autocratic
- ☐ Democratic
- ☐ Laissez-faire

New Product Development
1. Idea Generation
2. Screening of Ideas
3. Concept Development
4. Feasibility Study
5. Prototype Development
6. Test Marketing
7. Full Launch

MONITORING THE BUSINESS

Gross Profit Percentage:

$$\frac{\text{Gross Profit} \times 100}{\text{Sales}}$$

Net Profit Percentage:

$$\frac{\text{Net Profit} \times 100}{\text{Sales}}$$

Return On Investment:

$$\frac{\text{Net Profit} \times 100}{\text{Balance Sheet Total}}$$

Current Ratio:

$$\frac{\text{Current Assets}}{\text{Current Liabilities}}$$

Acid Test Ratio:

$$\frac{\text{Current Assets Less Closing Stock}}{\text{Current Liabilities}}$$

Debt Equity Ratio:

$$\frac{\text{Long-term Debt}}{\text{Issued Ordinary Shares} + \text{Reserves}}$$

Marketing Mix
- ☐ Product
- ☐ Price
- ☐ Place
- ☐ Promotion

Promotional Mix
- ☐ Advertising
- ☐ Sales Promotion
- ☐ Public Relations and Sponsorship
- ☐ Personal Selling